3.00

Educational
Environments
No. 3

Educational
Environments
No. 3

Roger Yee

Visual Reference Publications Inc., New York

Opposite: University of Connecticut, Stamford Branch, Stamford, Connecticut. **Architect:** Perkins Eastman. **Photographer:** Chuck Choi.

Educational Environments No. 3

GROUP PUBLISHER	Larry Fuersich larry@visualreference.com
PUBLISHER	Bill Ash bill@visualreference.com
EDITORIAL DIRECTOR	Roger Yee yeerh@aol.com
CREATIVE ART DIRECTOR	Veronika Cherepanina veronika@visualreference.com
CIRCULATION MANAGER	Amy Yip amy@visualreference.com
PRODUCTION MANAGER	John Hogan johnhvrp@yahoo.com
MARKETING COORDINATOR	Nika Chopra nika@visualreference.com
CONTROLLER	Angie Goulimis angie@visualreference.com

Visual Reference Publications, Inc.
302 Fifth Avenue
New York, NY 10001
Tel: 212.279.7000 • Fax: 212.279.7014

www.visualreference.com

Distributors to the trade in the United States and Canada
Watson-Guptill
770 Broadway
New York, NY 10003

Distributors outside the United States and Canada
HarperCollins International
10 East 53rd Street
New York, NY 10022-5299

Library of Congress Cataloging in Publication Data:
Educational Environments No. 3

Printed in China

ISBN: 978-1-58471-102-5

Book Design: Veronika Cherepanina

It's not what
you think.

It's Acrovyn.

KI...furniture for high-performance learning environments!

Educational focus. Award-winning innovation. The broadest offering. Chosen by more schools worldwide. KI...positively the recognized expert in educational furniture.

For all areas...classrooms to lecture halls, libraries to cafeterias, computer labs to residence halls, offices to laboratories... anywhere you need a partner with specialized expertise in the education market, look to KI. Only KI researches, develops and builds award-winning furniture solutions that enhance and withstand the rigors of high-performance learning environments.

Contact the experts at 1-800-424-2432 or visit kieducation.com.

Style.
Composition.
Harmony.

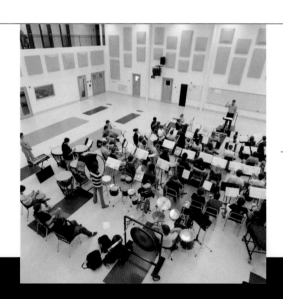

Create a design that really performs.

For over 60 years, Wenger has focused on specialty areas like the music wing, auditoriums, theatres and athletic spaces. We've helped establish effective design guidelines and tools for acoustics, layout, traffic flow, storage and more. And we've consulted with architects and educators on thousands of projects to create cost-effective environments that work. When it comes to creating high-performance speciality areas, Wenger is your leading resource. Call us – we are ready to assist with a series of planning tools and experienced representatives.

Your Performance Partner

Contents

*I*ntroduction

Every Child Above Average

*D*o you know where Mercedes-Benz M-Class SUVs are made? Alabama. And Apple i-Pods? China. You're confused? Blame it on globalization. Most of us are only vaguely aware of who produces our goods and services.

Americans can draw an unambiguous message from the confusion, however. The United States now competes with nations whose young, well-educated and ambitious workers earn less for work of equal quality and sophistication. To retain economic leadership, our nation must give students a good education.

Judging from the Program for International Student Assessment, an international survey conducted by the Organization for Economic Cooperation and Development (OECD) that measure 15-year-olds' capabilities in reading literacy, mathematics literacy and science literacy every three years, American students have room for improvement. The U.S. average score in reading literacy was not measurably different from the OECD average in 2003. Worse, U.S. scores in mathematics and science literacy were significantly lower than OECD averages.

In fairness, the nation has made repeated efforts to remedy educational deficiencies. The landmark No Child Left Behind Act of 2001, for example, was based on accountability for results. Unfortunately, its results are problematic, owing to such factors as continuing federal and state disagreements over educational policy.

But progress is being made. Work on needed school construction, encompassing new construction, additions, and renovation, is continuing nationwide to the tune of $21.6 billion in 2005 and $20.2 billion projected for 2006. New, smaller schools and schools with smaller classes have reported encouraging results. Public and private schools are separating K-12 grades into lower and upper forms to create more supportive learning environments for multiple learning styles. Public schools are learning to share facilities with communities.

Thus, this is no time to ease up on the pursuit of excellence among the nation's 49.6 million K-12 students or 16.6 million college and university students. That Americans remain committed to a strong educational system can be seen in the superb new educational facilities, designed by leading architects and interior designers, depicted in the following pages. What these facilities tell us is that America's children can indeed be leaders in the 21st century.

Roger Yee
Editor

VS

CREATIVE FURNITURE SOLUTIONS FOR EDUCATIONAL ENVIRONMENTS

VS America, Inc.:
1940 Abbott Street, Unit 501
Charlotte, NC 28203
Phone: 704-378-6500
Fax: 704-378-6005

info@vs-furniture.com
www.vs-furniture.com

VS International, Germany:
P.O. Box 1420
97934 Tauberbischofsheim
Phone: +49-9341-88888
Fax: +49-9341-88230

vsexport@vs-moebel.de
www.vs-furniture.com

BAR Architects

543 Howard Street
San Francisco, CA 94105
415.293.5700
415.293.5701 (Fax)
www.bararch.com

BAR Architects

BAR Architects

University of California, Santa Cruz
Infill Apartments
Santa Cruz, California

Above: Porter College exterior at dusk.

Right: Stevenson College residential complex.

Bottom right: Porter College residential complex.

Opposite: Cowell College residential complex.

Photography: © Douglas Dun/ BAR Architects.

Distinguished for academic programs that prepare many of its undergraduates to earn doctorates, the University of California, Santa Cruz (UCSC) continues to grow 41 years after its founding. The current enrollment of 15,000 students is projected to reach 19,500 by 2020. However, UCSC is taking care to preserve the strong sense of community and the distinctive relationship its ten residential colleges bring to their spectacular 2,000-acre campus. Recently completed infill apartments for three of the original colleges—Cowell, Stevenson, and Porter—designed by BAR Architects, reaffirm

the school's commitment to architectural excellence and environmental awareness. Designed to blend with the appearance of the original colleges, the 701-bed facilities, totalling 235,150 square feet of new construction, added 67,750 to Cowell, 51,000 to Stevenson, and 116,000 to Porter. They introduced new concepts in student apartment living, multi-use, lounges and common areas, kitchenettes, central laundries, and computer laboratories. What is especially impressive about these handsome, high-density residential units is their ability to add to the vitality of their colleges while preserv-

ing many of the existing trees and views, and nurturing an environment for a rich student life within low-cost constraints. No less notable are such green building features as site positioning for solar shading and photovoltaic panels, green finish materials, and storm water mitigation measures, which give the impressive architecture a beauty that goes much deeper than its façade.

BAR Architects

University of California, Davis
Tercero Dining Commons
Davis, California

Students seem to forget the usual clichés about college dorms when they enter the new Tercero Dining Commons at the University of California, Davis, one of America's top research universities. Who wouldn't? Gone is the traditional cook, serve, eat routine. BAR Architects renovated the original 38,500-square foot dining commons built in 1965 and designed a new, two-story, 28,000-square foot addition—transforming the austere, concrete dining commons, into an open, inviting, and visually coherent contemporary building. The rejuvenated and expanded Commons, located in the Tercero Residential District on the 5,300-acre UC Davis campus, now serves 2,400 students in a space that includes four distinct dining areas offering marketplace-style serving platforms and seating for 900, a full-service bakery, free-standing 1,600-square foot snack shop/convenience store and ample outdoor dining. The reborn Tercero Dining Commons also functions as a student center, providing a residential lounge, academic advising center, administrative offices, study areas, computer laboratory and mail services. With warm interiors comprised of ceramic tile, stained concrete, anigre ceiling panels, cherry and Douglas fir millwork, and a sensitive mixture of steel, concrete, aluminum curtainwall, cedar wood trellises and metal panels on the exterior facades, Tercero Dining Commons demonstrates what happen when a university and its architect get serious about students' quality of life on campus.

Above: Exterior night view west dining room.

Top right: Serving Station.

Top Middle Right: West dining room seating.

Top Far Right: Façade.

Opposite: Exterior day view.

Photography: © Douglas Dun/BAR Architects.

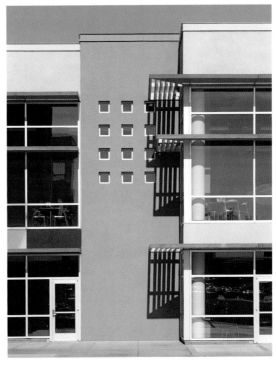

BAR Architects

University of California, Berkeley
Clark Kerr Dining Commons
Berkeley, California

At first glance, you might overlook the impact of the historic building rehabilitation on the landmark, Spanish Mission-style Clark Kerr Campus at the University of California, Berkeley, so sensitive is the design by BAR Architects. However, the restored, one-story, 23,000-square-foot dining commons has undergone extensive changes. In order for the building to function as a major conference center as well as a student dining facility, the architect has reorganized the internal circulation and connections to outdoor dining, created an all new light-filled servery, revived two exterior courtyards into beautiful multi-use "outdoor rooms," upgraded all interior finishes, added new structural bracing and building systems, refurbished historic light fixtures while adding compatible new fixtures and restored functionality to the antiquated kitchen and back of house areas. The effort has culminated in a revitalized, 800-seat dining facility that also offers multiple conference and private dining opportunities. Furthermore, this popular student hub showcases environmentally friendly details such as sustainable flooring, improved interior acoustics, applied films over historic glazing to reflect sunlight, non-VOC paint, high efficiency lamps in the restored light fixtures and many other green finish materials. It's a welcome change for the 818 students on the Clark Kerr Campus, as well as the latest milestone for a complex originally built as a K-12 school for the deaf and blind in the 1920's.

Top Left: Entry arcade and hall towards main dining room.

Top right: Servery from east courtyard.

Right: Servery.

Opposite: Main dining room.

Photography: © Douglas Dun/BAR Architects.

15

BAR Architects

Sonoma State University
Music Education Complex, Green Music Center
Rohnert Park, California

The performing arts, music education and fine dining will be an integrated experience at the Donald and Maureen Green Music Center at Sonoma State University. The Center, located on the 46-year-old, 269-acre campus in Sonoma County, will enrich the intellectual, artistic and cultural life of the Wine Country and the Bay Area. During the academic year, the Santa Rosa Symphony and the Department of Music, with its strong instrumental, vocal and jazz programs, will share the facilities; in the summer, the Green Music Festival will bring world-class artists to audiences of up to 15,000 people and the Center will offer music and theater workshops at Greenfarm, an educational arts program for students of all ages. The two-story, 101,250-square-foot Center is composed of three buildings organized around the Festival Lawn, courtyards and gardens. The Music Education Building, designed by BAR Architects features a 250-seat Recital Hall that is ideal for organ and choral music; numerous rehearsal and ensemble rooms; practice rooms, classrooms and administrative offices.

The BAR-designed Hospitality Center includes a 300-seat restaurant with gardens for weddings and receptions, conference rooms, gift shop and support spaces for performers. The 1,400-seat Concert Hall, designed by William Rawn Associates, completes the complex. The Center's 2008 opening will unveil an exciting environment where students and professionals, audience and performers can come together for music, cultural events, and of course, fine wine.

Bergmeyer Associates, Inc.

51 Sleeper Street
Boston, MA 02210-1208
617.542.1025
617.542.1026 (Fax)
www.bergmeyer.com
info@bergmeyer.com

Bergmeyer Associates, Inc.

Bergmeyer Associates, Inc.

Salem State College
Central Campus Residence Hall
Salem, Massachusetts

Top left: Seminar room.
Top right: Student bedroom.
Above: Kitchen in residential suite.

Above right: Lounge.
Opposite: Exterior at main entrance.
Photography: Lucy Chen.

A new, 438-bed, four-story, 142,000-square-foot Central Campus Residence Hall, designed by Bergmeyer Associates Inc., has opened to receive students and enhance campus life at Salem State College—a thriving, coeducational institution of 8,790 students in Salem, Massachusetts that dates back to 1854. The new student residence, planned with student and faculty participation, offers 75 six-person, apartment-style student suites, one residential staff unit, two graduate assistant studios, and two faculty apartments, and is the new focal point for the school's 37.5-acre Central Campus. To nurture an academic community within its walls, the facility incorporates study areas, a well-equipped seminar room, and an extensive, first-floor lounge offering fitness, laundry, pool tables and other games, as well as adjacent academic and administrative offices. Outside, the building uses its long, low form and H-shaped layout to frame views of the campus's largest open green lawn to the west; and a tidal salt marsh and the Forest River to the east. Students in the first-floor lounge can look in both directions to survey the world around them, even as the building's Georgian brickwork evokes the heritage of historic Salem, founded in 1626, and its modern architecture looks ahead to the town's fourth century.

Bergmeyer Associates, Inc.

Northeastern University
Kerr Hall
Boston, Massachusetts

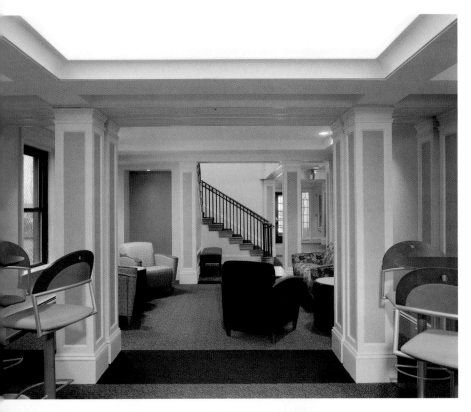

Steps from Fenway Park, home of the Boston Red Sox, stands a traditional, five-story, brick-clad residence hall with an unconventional past—and a bright future. Thanks to a recently completed, 24,000-square-foot renovation, designed by Bergmeyer Associates Inc., Kerr Hall has fully recovered from a disastrous gas explosion to resume its current mission—housing 119 students at Boston's Northeastern University. Originally constructed in 1917 as Students House, a cooperative home for women attending Boston area colleges and universities, Kerr Hall was purchased in 1972 by Northeastern for its own growing student population. Bergmeyer As-

sociates Inc. was chosen for the remodeling because their previous work on campus demonstrated an ability to cope with the project's tight, four-month deadline, collaborate with school personnel and balance historic preservation with innovative design. The renovation has focused chiefly on damaged areas, encompassing the common spaces and faculty dining facility on the first and second floors. While a new layout has transformed the first floor by opening up space without compromising security, upgraded finishes, warm colors and historically appropriate furnishings—inspired by the building's architectural detailing—have given the interiors

a fresh, timely feeling that simultaneously embraces and looks beyond nine decades of occupancy.

Top left: Lounge.

Top right: Lobby and reception desk.

Left: Stair hall.

Opposite: Corridor to dining room.

Photography: Lucy Chen.

20

Bergmeyer Associates, Inc. with Jonathan Levi Architects

Harvard University
29 Garden Street
Cambridge, Massachusetts

If Harvard University's graduate students suspect that undergraduates lead a charmed life they are denied, buoyed by such amenities as sumptuous, neo-Georgian houses built by the school in the 1930s, they have some justification. Most graduate students must rent off-campus housing in greater Boston's tight and costly housing market. But a measure of relief has arrived. The renovation of 29 Garden Street, in Cambridge, has transformed a former hotel into a five-level, 114,000-square-foot graduate student and faculty residence with 74 dwelling units and 148 beds, designed by Jonathan Levi Architects with Bergmeyer Associates Inc. to invest the building with an environment conducive to the lifestyles of today's graduate students. The design has produced a variety of bright and airy contemporary units, including single-person studios, double studios, and two- and three-bedroom apartments, all featuring attractive kitchens and built-in shelves, tables and desks in birch veneer, introduced a formal, three-story, curtain wall-framed entry. They established a European-style, semi-public, landscaped courtyard atop a previously unused garage roof deck as a gathering place, and gave faculty apartments direct access to the courtyard to bring faculty and students together. Graduate school life may never resemble the undergraduate experience at Harvard, but 29 Garden Street delivers more than hope.

Left: New entrance.
Bottom left: Ground floor lobby.
Opposite top: Evening view.
Opposite: Exterior and courtyard garden.
Photography: Peter Vanderwarker.

Bergmeyer Associates, Inc.

Salem State College
Peabody and Bowditch Halls
Salem, Massachusetts

Above: Café, Peabody Hall.
Top right: Lobby, Bowditch Hall.
Above right: Lounge, Bowditch Hall.
Left: Kitchen, Peabody Hall.
Photography: Lucy Chen.

Parents with rosy memories of student dormitory life decades ago are often unprepared for what today's college and university students expect—and receive—as campus housing. Where students spend some 20 percent of their time on campus has become another competitive event in the annual collegiate tournament to snare the best and brightest high school seniors. For schools like Salem State College, in Salem, Massachusetts, the introduction of new, state-of-the-art student residences is frequently accompanied by the upgrading of existing ones. Consider Salem State's successful renovation of two nearly identical 1960s-era, corridor-style residence halls, 370-bed Peabody Hall and 300-bed Bowditch Hall, designed by Bergmeyer Associates Inc., architect of the school's new Central Campus Residence Hall. In a highly visible makeover, new elevators have been installed within new external towers that not only replace unreliable elevators, they mitigate the buildings' bland, dated appearance with their massing and new, adjacent glass-lined vestibules that act as distinctive "front doors." Inside, the bedrooms, kitchens, restrooms, lobbies and hallways have benefited from vibrant new colors, upgraded finishes, and comfortable modern furnishings that are stylish as well as durable. Students increasingly want schools to offer a home away from home, and institutions like Salem State are clearly paying attention.

Booth Hansen

333 S.Desplaines
Chicago, IL 60661
312.869.5000
312.869.5099 (Fax)
www.boothhansen.com

Booth Hansen

Booth Hansen

Kohl Children's Museum
Glenview, Illinois

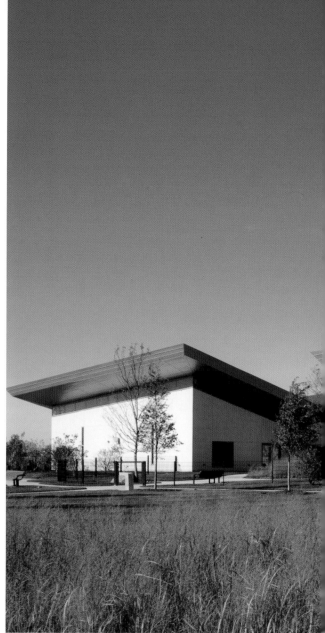

See Dick crawl...through a labyrinth! See Jane build... her own house! Now, parents and educators in the greater Chicago area of Illinois have an appealing new way to introduce children to the role of interactive play in learning: the recently completed, two-floor, 48,000-square-foot Kohl Children's Museum on an 8.8-acre site in Glenview, designed by Booth Hansen. In relocating from Wilmette to The Glen, a mixed-use development at the former Glenview Naval Air Station, the Museum was developed with extensive participation by Museum representatives and the Glenview Redevelopment Committee to meet the Museum's programmatic

goals, acknowledge the Village of Glenview's architectural guidelines, satisfy environmental design objectives, and accommodate families, school groups and visitors of diverse backgrounds and abilities. The resulting facility, encompassing indoor and outdoor interactive exhibits, store/café, performance space, classrooms, administrative offices and support space, forms a village-like aggregation of rectangular volumes under a sculptural metal roof of gables and inverted "V" shapes. The interior captures daylight from a continuous band of clerestory windows and a few, strategically placed picture windows that bring light and views into the

largely open exhibit areas. Museum president Sheridan Turner calls the award-winning design, "the perfect architectural reflection of our values and mission."

Top left: Reception.
Above: Evening view of entrance.
Top right: Exterior.
Right: Interior.
Opposite bottom right: Interior.
Photography: Mark Ballogg.

Booth Hansen

The School of the Art Institute of Chicago
162 North State Street Residences
Chicago, Illinois

Right: State Street perspective.

Bottom right: Elevation at grade along Randolph Street showing Old Heidelberg Restaurant façade.

Opposite: View from Daley Plaza with Picasso sculpture in foreground.

Photography: Nick Merrick/ Hedrich Blessing.

You won't find ivy-covered quadrangles at the School of the Art Institute of Chicago. Since this prestigious independent art school, founded in 1866 and once ranked by *U.S. News & World Report* as America's "best art school," has no formal grounds, its 2,554 students consider the Loop, the heart of downtown Chicago, their campus. Its two residence halls, for example, place students in bustling urban settings. One, the Chicago Building, is a 1904 landmark, designed by Holabird and Roche and adapted

to student residences by Booth Hansen. The other, the recently completed 500-bed, 300,000-square-foot 162 North State Street Residences, also designed by Booth Hansen, is a multi-purpose renovation and addition, combining studio apartments, solarium, studio work spaces, exercise room, computer lounge, study room, television lounge and laundry facilities with an 11,000-square-foot Gene Siskel Film Center, an 8,500-square-foot repertory theater, 35,000 square feet of retail space, and the historic façade of the former Old Heidelberg

Restaurant. The exterior resolves the complexity of renovating an existing 16-story building and combining it with a new 17-story addition by creating a contemporary interpretation of the Chicago School of Architecture, complete with bay windows and a deep, overhanging cornice, linking it to the past and future of its dynamic site.

Booth Hansen

Moraine Valley Community College
Palos Hills, Illinois

Do motivated students just need good educational opportunities to succeed, with little concern for the spaces where they study? That's not how Moraine Valley Community College, in Palos Hills, Illinois, works. In fact, it could be argued that the school's faith in design explains why it stands 94th in rankings for associate degrees conferred out of 1,173 community colleges nationwide, why 87 percent of its occupational graduates find employment, or even why so many graduates—98 percent—would "recommend Moraine Valley to a friend." Consider its new, two-floor, 60,000-square foot building, designed by Booth Hansen, which comprises 32 classrooms, seminar rooms, faculty offices, bookstore/ cyber café and administrative offices. Constructed with long-span structural trusses to minimize the columns and foundations in an unstable soil environment, the building is configured to create an effective learning atmosphere that promotes a feeling of community among 46,000 students representing widely ranging ages and lifestyles. How so? The scheme wraps the two levels of freestanding classrooms and offices around the two-story book-store/cyber café, treats the major corridor as an easily navigable indoor "street," and fills interiors with daylight and views of the campus and surrounding prairie. It's as complex—and simple— as that.

Right: Cyber Cafe.
Below: Entrance.
Bottom: Exterior.
Photography: Doug Snower.

Booth Hansen

University of Illinois at Urbana-Champaign
Student Housing and Dining Complex
Champaign, Illinois

Student life at the University of Illinois at Urbana-Champaign should be significantly enriched with the completion of two key projects, the Student Dining and Residential Programs Building (SDRP) and Residence Hall One, both designed by Booth Hansen. The two-story, 140,000-square-foot SDRP replaces two existing dining facilities to serve over 3,600 students in three venues —the Marketplace, the Emporium and the Coffeehouse— acknowledging wide-ranging student tastes with a variety of cuisines, carry-out service, and different settings. Besides being the largest student dining center on campus, the SDRP will also contain meeting and group study facilities for neighborhood residents,

office space for student organizations, a learning commons and accommodations for large group events. Residence Hall One, a 500-bed, five-story, 132,000-square-foot facility, is the first in a series of student residences to be replaced as part of the campus master plan. This new facility will house first- and second-year students in double-occupancy rooms with semi-private bathrooms, along with common lobbies, lounges and meeting rooms, a first-floor resident director's apartment, and units for students with severe physical disabilities. The two projects should help attract prospective students, as well as lift the spirits of nearly 42,000 students now attending the 139-year-old University.

Booth Hansen

Roosevelt University
Ganz Hall
Chicago, Illinois

Above: Detail of "electrolier."

Right: Perspective along main axis showing stage.

Bottom right: Side aisle with arcade and stained glass lunettes.

Photography: Greg Murphey.

Two years after its founding in 1945, Chicago's Roosevelt University, an independent, nonsectarian, coeducational institution, moved into the Auditorium Building, the 1890 masterpiece by architects Dankmar Adler and Louis Sullivan. The school's pragmatic yet respectful approach to the landmark building still prevails over a half-century later in the restoration of Ganz Hall by Booth Hansen. The 200-seat, 4,000-square-foot recital hall, located on the seventh floor, was originally designed as a banquet hall by Adler,

Sullivan and their apprentice Frank Lloyd Wright. Constructed a year after the completion of the building, Ganz Hall was resplendent in plaster and carved wood ornament, gold-leaf stenciled arches supported by tiger maple wood columns with hand-carved wooden capitals, stained glass lunette windows, and stunning electric chandeliers. Over time, the grandeur of the hall was lost, the beautiful electric chandeliers replaced by large white globes, and the details of the room faded. To restore the space and adapt it for

use as a modern recital hall, Booth Hansen selected new seats, added an acoustically-balanced mechanical system, and reconfigured the room to accommodate a stage and back-of-house facilities. Most dramatic, however, was the recreation of the original cast-iron "electroliers," based on extensive study of archival photographs. Even the light bulbs are authentic, being replicas of the original Edison carbon filament lamps that cast the warm, golden light beloved by Adler, Sullivan and Wright.

Bruner/Cott

130 Prospect Street
Cambridge, MA 02139
617.492.8400
617.876.4002 (Fax)
www.brunercott.com

Bruner/Cott

Bruner/Cott

University of Chicago
Bartlett Dining Commons
Chicago, Illinois

Where University of Chicago students once assembled in devotion "To the advancement of Physical Education and the Glory of Manly Sports," at Frank Dickinson Bartlett Gymnasium, built in 1901, they currently gather to confront such culinary challenges as The Diner (home-style cooking), Harvest (vegan and vegetarian), Flavors of Asia (Malaysian, Chinese, Thai and Japanese cuisine) and other food stations anchoring their 211-acre campus's newest dining facility. The conversion of Bartlett Gymnasium into Bartlett Dining Commons, a 550-seat, three-story, 64,300-square-foot foodservice facility, designed by Bruner/Cott, introduces such new uses as dining rooms, exhibition cooking servery, production kitchen and storage, 10,000 square feet of space for events, performances, offices and lounges, as well as complex new infrastructure required for contemporary occupancy and code requirements. Remnants of the former gym persist, including the historic running track, now a lounge and observation deck. But the new, award-winning design is establishing its own identity through such activities as the Maroon Market, a convenience store open until 2:00 a.m. every day. John D. Rockefeller, who founded the University in 1890, would probably have been impressed at the "Bart Mart's" success in satisfying student cravings for Ben & Jerry's ice cream, flavored coffees and pizza.

Top left: Former running track is now a mezzanine lounge.

Top right: Exterior.

Above right: Dining hall as seen from mezzanine.

Right: Servery in operation.

Opposite: Evening view of servery.

Photography: Peter Vanderwarker, Hedrich Blessing.

Bruner/Cott

Harvard University
University Hall
Cambridge, Massachusetts

Visitors to Harvard University's venerable Yard always pause at University Hall, a Neoclassical icon designed in 1813 by Charles Bulfinch, architect of the Massachusetts State House and primary architect of the United States Capitol, and the revered statue of John Harvard, created in 1885 by Daniel Chester French, sculptor of the Lincoln Memorial, that stands before it. Of course, as one of the older structures housing America's first institution of higher education (1636), University Hall showed its age. Not only had much of Bulfinch's stately interior been partitioned and otherwise compromised, its granite exterior was spalling, one of four monumental entry stairs sagged, no door was accessible to wheelchairs, air conditioners protruded from windows, and windows and frames no longer matched. In a recent restoration and modernization of the four-story, 30,000-square-foot landmark, Bruner/Cott has reconstructed Bulfinch's architecture and updated it with concealed ramps, lifts and elevator for universal access, all-new mechanical and electrical systems, and significant structural repairs. While the restoration of Bulfinch's two-story high College Chapel returned it to its glory in 1896 as the Faculty Room, the space symbolizes what has been done for the entire building, reviving its original character for modern occupants to use and enjoy.

Top left: Exterior, Harvard Yard.

Top right: Hallway features original Bulfinch brick floor and granite staircase.

Above: Faculty room.

Opposite: Entry lobby and updated office space.

Photography: Peter Vanderwarker.

Bruner/Cott
with Johnson Johnson Crabtree Architects

Vanderbilt University
Sarratt Student Center
Nashville, Tennessee

An internationally respected research institution based in Nashville, Tennessee, Vanderbilt University long ago exceeded the goal set by Commodore Cornelius Vanderbilt, who founded it in 1873 to "contribute to strengthening the ties that should exist between all sections of our common country." Vanderbilt's ongoing commitment to excellence—*U.S. News & World Report* ranks the school among America's top 20 universities—also helps it avoid complacency. Consider how the school dealt with the underused student center serving some 11,000 students on its 313-acre campus. To develop the new, two-story, 70,000-square-

foot Sarratt Student Center, designed by Bruner/Cott in association with Johnson Johnson Crabtree, Vanderbilt invited the designers to involve students, faculty and staff in focus groups and interviews that identified numerous specific needs for a successful building program. The Center's resulting blend of renovation and new construction combines Vanderbilt's main dining hall, art gallery, performance spaces, art studios, bookstore, mailroom, cinema, pub, study areas, administrative offices and meeting space for 50 student organizations. Reorganizing three formerly separate buildings around a new core space entered through a light-filled atrium, the facility integrates old and new to produce an effective, inviting and popular student center that genuinely functions as a center for student life.

Below: Entry lobby.
Bottom right: Courtyard.
Bottom left: Student-run art gallery and reception desk.
Opposite: Entrance and addition.
Photography: Eric Lafevor.

Bruner/Cott

Harvard University
Harvard Dance Center
Cambridge, Massachusetts

With 23 dance companies residing on a campus where rehearsal space has often been small and inadequately equipped, Harvard University's Dance Program recently moved into what might be considered a dream come true—the Harvard Dance Center at the Quadrangle Recreational Activities Center, in Cambridge, designed by Bruner/Cott. The one-level, 35,400-square-foot facility comprises a 4,100-square-foot main dance studio equipped with overhead skylights, 400 square feet of mirrors, custom-designed flooring, a full technical booth, and a wall of tiered seating for an audience of 200, as well as a second, 1,100-square-foot studio, offices, dressing rooms and a green room. To create it, a stand-alone structure was inserted within an existing multi-purpose gymnasium space, existing mechanical and electrical systems were upgraded, and separate exterior entrances and identities were provided for the Dance Program and remaining athletic activities at QRAC. How does the new studio function? "Working with Bruner/Cott and Alan Symonds (Harvard lighting designer), our goal was to create a space that works equally well for performance, classes and rehearsals, and converts quickly among these uses," notes Elizabeth Bergmann, dance director at Harvard's Office for the Arts. "The result is one of the best spaces I've seen in my career."

Above right: Rehearsal room.
Right: Wall of mirrors.
Below: Theater with auditorium seating.
Photography: Peter Vanderwarker.

Cannon Design

Cannon Design

Cannon Design

James Madison School of Excellence
Rochester, New York

Enlisting a village to raise a child is not a metaphor at award-winning James Madison School of Excellence, in Rochester, New York, designed by Cannon Design. Developed to alleviate overcrowding at existing schools, the two-story, 185,000-square-foot facility accommodates 1,000 students in grades 6-8. Madison goes well beyond raising capacity by creating a fully-integrated Community Center, addressing neighborhood concerns about size, noise and location, arranging spaces to minimize travel distance and maximize educational time, and nurturing a special and positive environment through such amenities as a formal entry court, a commons that serves as a "town square," and classroom blocks that establish four "houses" of 250 students who remain together for common activities such as lunch or gym. A curved wall defines the two-story, skylit "street" connecting all the school's major elements. The academic houses and science elements line one side of the curve, defining the formal entry court, while dining, library,

lecture and athletic facilities frame the opposite side, facing the playing fields. Zoned separately yet sharing facilities, the Community Center functions as a hub for social services, providing remedial and continuing education and organized recreational and sports activities that welcome students and local residents alike.

Top right: Library.
Above: Entry into student street.
Right: Student street.
Below right: Lecture hall.
Opposite: Student street.
Photography: Tim Wilkes Photography.

Cannon Design

Middle/Senior High School
Chester, New York

Top right: Auditorium is a shared function.

Right: Main entrance.

Opposite: The project establishes a visual connection to the natural environment.

Opposite bottom left: Dining facility has a full teaching kitchen.

Opposite bottom right: Library is infused with natural light.

Photography: Tim Wilkes Photography.

Should 1000 junior and senior high school students mix? Early in the development of Chester Union Free School District's new Middle/Senior High School, in Chester, New York, planners realized the two student populations required physical separation and a clear sense of physical identity. Accordingly, the award-winning, three-story, 125,000-square-foot facility, designed by Cannon Design, provides two distinct classroom wings, separated by a lobby and common areas. Inside the red brick walls, which evoke a traditional school image, a "village" of contrasting architectural elements identifies shared functions—gymnasium, cafeteria and auditorium—that encircle a "plaza" and double as community resources for this farming community of some 13,000 residents. Within the wings, various classroom types incorporate atypically large spaces for classroom computers as well as generous outdoor views. In fact, a strong visual connection to the natural environment and maximum use of daylighting prevail throughout the school in response to the site—an open field adjacent to the existing elementary school. Occupying a terrain of plateaus and retaining walls crossed by a wetland stream and public bike trail and flanked by forested hillsides, the school represents what the Society of American Registered Architects calls "an inviting setting for education."

Cannon Design

Cornwall Central High School
Cornwall on Hudson, New York

Top Left: Connecting bridge at night.

Right: Diagonal glass trestle connects public and private space.

Bottom left: Library/media center.

Bottom right Gallery overlooks the art classroom.

Photography: Tim Wilkes Photography.

The new Cornwall Central High School in Cornwall on Hudson, New York, could dissuade parents of its 1000 students from yearning for the "good old days." This striking, three-story, 218,000-square-foot building, designed by Cannon Design, does more than alleviate overcrowded, antiquated facilities and meet rigorous standards recently adopted by New York State. Its state-of-the-art environment provides audio, video and data to all classrooms; student spaces for socialization and studying; athletic facilities such as tennis courts and indoor pool; 1,000-seat auditorium and media center/library, all within a modern architectural context that makes inspired use of a Hudson Valley hillside. Acknowledging the region's rolling topography and railroad trestle bridges, the design strategically uses the steepest part of the site to locate two linear "bars" that minimize the need for excavation and frame the courtyard/amphitheater, reserving the flatter areas for playfields. The interiors are as exciting as they are effective, including classroom corridors that reflect a "train track" rhythm, recessed gym and pool volumes that are capped by a gently curving roofline echoing the hills beyond, and a diagonal glass "trestle" that connects public and private spaces, culminating in a cantilevered media center reading room with spectacular Hudson Valley views.

Cannon Design

Stephen & Harriet Myers Middle School
Albany, New York

What could be more appropriate for the Albany City School District than to open the Stephen & Harriet Myers Middle School, in Albany, New York, to students of all ages through continuing education, in addition to some 650 students grades in 6-8? The new, three-story, 140,400-square-foot school, designed by Cannon Design, is organized so students and community can share such precious resources as a competition gymnasium with spectator seating, 25-yard swimming pool and locker rooms, 650-seat auditorium with performance stage, atrium, library, cafeteria, and over 40 classrooms accommodating such subjects as science, technology, art, consumer science and chorus. Acoustical control was especially important given the variety of programmatic spaces and the potential for noise to impact adjoining learning areas. Consider its major organizing element, the monumental, three-story, 40-foot-high by 245-foot-long atrium that links major spaces and functions as a forum for encounter and interaction. To promote openness and minimize reverberation, the atrium is capped by a unique, V-shaped ceiling whose profile of varying lengths and angles disrupts sounds at the upper levels and dampens noise levels overall. With intrusive noise isolated from teaching areas, Myers Middle School can clearly hear and fulfill the needs of its diverse student population.

Top left: Acoustical panels enhance sound control.

Top right: Exterior.

Above Gymnasium.

Photography: Tim Wilkes Photography.

Cannon Design

Joseph E. Hill Education Center
Evanston, Illinois

Top right: Exterior looking into community boardroom.

Right: Recycled auto tires provide a soft, resilient playground surface.

Bottom right: Public lobby and reception desk.

Photography: Hedrich Blessing.

At first glance, the activities within Evanston/Skokie School District #65's new Joseph E. Hill Education Center, in Evanston, Illinois, may seem unrelated: pre-school, pre-primary special education, adult education and district administration. However, the consolidation of these groups in a single, two-story, 224,000-square-foot facility attests to the District's commitment to an integrated system of education for the Evanston/Skokie community in suburban Chicago. The organization of the Center, designed by Cannon Design, readily supports its components with a two-story public lobby that provides direct, ground-floor access to the community boardroom, Family Focus adult education program with associated childcare facilities, early childhood and pre-primary special education school, and the Evanston School Children's Clothing Association, which distributes clothing to families in need. Upstairs, administrative functions share space with the Jordan Teachers' Center, a professional development and resource library for District faculty and staff, that encourages interaction between administrative and teaching staffs. The Center is a good neighbor as well, due to its sustainable design and building material palette of brick, stone, metal and glass, complementing a neighboring District school building. And for the finishing touch, silk-screened student artwork from the District's 16 schools adorns the curving window wall facing the street.

CBT

110 Canal Street
Boston, MA 02114-1805
617.262.4354
617.267.9667 (Fax)
www.cbtarchitects.com

CBT

CBT

St. Mark's School
Center for the Arts
Southborough, Massachusetts

Since its founding in 1865, an enduring sense of community has sustained St. Mark's School, a college-preparatory boarding and day school for 325 students, grades 9-12, in Southborough, Massachusetts. Indeed, the new, 32,000-square-foot Center for the Arts, designed by CBT, intertwines old and new to reaffirm communal values: a 500-seat concert hall and music rehearsal space in a new building, a renovated Taft Hall for the visual arts, a 200-seat studio theater for the dramatic arts in a building that contained outdated handball courts and a multi-purpose space in Benson Hall, a 1910 former gymnasium. The Center creates a new academic quadrangle along primary circulation paths crossing the 250-acre campus, acknowledging that the new concert hall can accommodate daily morning meetings for students and faculty. It occupies a perimeter site near the main road to minimize the concert hall's bulk, and surrounds this volume with a one- and two-story mass containing practice and music classrooms to reduce overall visual impact and integrate the new quadrangle with the existing campus. A thoroughly modern structure in function, the Center celebrates a timeless community with such traditional campus elements as brick, precast concrete, slate roof, copper metalwork, bay windows and whimsical towers.

Top left: Rehearsal room.

Top right: Lobby.

Above: Exterior.

Opposite: Stage view of concert hall.

Photography: Robert Benson.

CBT

The success of Brandeis University's Graduate School of International Economics and Finance was apparent soon after its 1994 opening. With students responding enthusiastically to the School's highly rated program, enrollment surged and its facilities on the 235-acre Brandeis campus, in Waltham, Massachusetts, were quickly filled. Thus, the recent arrival of the new, 24,000-square-foot Lemberg Academic Center, designed by CBT, has improved conditions appreciably for 500 undergraduate and 250 graduate students, nearly doubling the size of the 1972 Sachar International Center, which houses

the School. To integrate the two structures, the new interior, comprising three state-of-the-art classrooms, faculty offices, conference rooms, meeting areas and cyber café, is enclosed in an exterior of metal, brick and glass that ties it to the older building, and is connected by pedestrian bridges that are popular gathering places. The design also satisfies the School's goal of encouraging collaboration and intellectual exchange through such common areas as the double-height World Court cyber café, where students can mingle or work in teams, and an adjacent conference room, designed for presenta-

tions and conferences for 14-20 people. There will be abundant activity in the new space, since phase two of the project will add residential space for 110 students.

Top left: Meeting area.
Top right: Exterior.
Above right: Classroom.
Right: Overlooking World Court.
Opposite: The World Court.
Photography: Robert Benson.

CBT

Pennsylvania State University
Eastview Terrace
State College, Pennsylvania

Upperclassmen say they can't find campus housing with privacy, independence and amenities. What's a school to do? Pennsylvania State University's new Eastview Terrace, an 811-bed, seven-building residential complex designed by CBT in association with Hayes Large Architects, provides an inspiring reply. The brick-clad, two- to four-story, 300,000-square-foot, Collegiate Georgian-style residence for upperclassmen, presenting a new quadrangle along the southeast edge of the 16,000-acre University Park campus in State College, features independent living environments with quality amenities that meet or exceed what students seek in off-campus housing. Replacing a series of 1940s housing units, Eastview Terrace establishes a strong sense of place by engaging its grounds fully through outdoor courtyards, generous terraces, a network of unobstructed pedestrian paths that flow around and through the buildings and a grand staircase that ascends the hill from the local community to the campus. Equally compelling is the interior environment, which encourages social and academic camaraderie while preserving individual privacy. Floors divided into open suites or "houses" of eight or 16 single bedrooms with private baths share such common spaces as living rooms/lounges, group study rooms, kitchenettes and laundries. Do upperclassmen appreciate the differences? Watch the crowds arriving in late August and early September.

Above: View of community terrace from great lawn.

Right: Community terrace and grand stair.

Opposite bottom left: Entry lounge.

Opposite bottom right: Common living room with group study.

Photography: Jonathan Hillyer.

Architect of Record: Hayes Large Architects.

Started as a part-time evening law school in 1898, Northeastern University knows its potential to help Boston's citizens. In fact, a recent example of its community outreach might be deemed a smashing success. The SquashBusters Badger and Rosen Facility is a three-story, 28,000-square-foot, state-of-the-art squash and fitness center, designed by CBT and jointly developed by Northeastern and SquashBusters, an after-school program that uses sports to provide mentorship and education opportunities to inner-city youth. On a 10,000-square-foot site beside an employee parking garage on the University's 67-acre campus and near a municipal playing field, the gently curving facility

manages to include eight squash courts, three class-rooms, office space, lockers and 8,000 square feet of fitness space. Not only does the modern glass, aluminum and concrete construction give SquashBusters its first permanent home since its founding in 1995, it surrounds its 400 students in a stimulating environment, highlighted by a triangular atrium, third-floor fitness center with an expansive window wall, and a glazed demonstration court that punches through the façade on the second floor above the entry. Not only does the demonstration court let pedestrians see champion-ship squash, it illuminates the neighborhood with light and energy at night.

Top left: SquashBusters at night.
Top right: Front façade.
Above: Squash courts.
Right: Atrium.
Photography: Robert Benson.

Champlin/Haupt Architects, Inc.

424 East Fourth Street
Cincinnati, OH 45202
513.241.4474
513.241.0081 (Fax)
all@charchitects.com
www.charchitects.com

Champlin/Haupt Architects, Inc.

Champlin/Haupt Architects, Inc.

Ohio State University at Lima and James A. Rhodes State College Life and Physical Sciences Center
Lima, Ohio

The Ohio State University touts 57,000 students on six campuses as part of its Big Ten reputation. Students on the smaller, 565 acre, regional Lima campus benefit from 'a world class education and an active student life with affordability.' Rhodes State College, West Central Ohio's largest two-year college, helping shape workforce development, partnered with OSU-Lima to bring science education to the region.

The new three-story 85,000 square-foot Life and Physical Sciences Center, designed by Champlin/Haupt Architects, enhances both institutions' reputation while allowing students and faculty to share an effective and stimulating learning environment. This award winning building consists of classrooms and laboratories for chemistry, biology, physics, geology and mathematics, along with a greenhouse, distance

learning center, and video production studio. Labs and teaching spaces are equipped to provide the flexibility necessary to evolve with the ever-changing nature of science education. The building employs racetrack corridors and a full-height lightwell to simplify wayfinding as well as create opportunities for informal student gathering. Outside, the building is a good neighbor, completing the original 1970s campus

quadrangle and incorporating glazed stair towers at both ends which become welcoming beacons at dusk.

Top left: Quadrangle entry.

Top right: Lightwell stair.

Above: Anatomy and physiology.

Below: Quadrangle facade.

Opposite: South view with stair and greenhouse.

Photography: Richard Loesch/ Camtech Photography.

Champlin/Haupt Architects, Inc.

Sinclair Community College
Library
Dayton, Ohio

One of the nation's largest community college campuses, serving over 110,000 individuals in college courses, training sessions and conferences, struggled for years with a hidden problem: its Library. Originally designed by Edward Durrell Stone, the Library at Sinclair Community College represented a vast underground space that was widely perceived as dark, confining and unattractive. Now, following a comprehensive renovation of the 66,000 square-foot main level and 29,500 square-foot loggia, designed by Champlin/Haupt Architects in conjunction with managing architect Alan Scherr Associates, the Library has been reestablished as a major focal point of campus life, providing technology, books, periodicals and other resources to students, faculty and community groups. The successful transformation has focused on visually lightening the existing architecture by painting the massive concrete ceiling plane white, replacing the previously monochromatic orange color scheme with a more sophisticated palette, and introducing natural materials and sizable splashes of color and texture to define zones of information and activity. Textured glass, accent tiles, maple wood trim and bright colors help make the stairway, circulation desk, and other major elements more appealing. A centrally located garden café with comfortable seating, large planters beneath refurbished skylights, abundant computer work stations and laptop portals make the space both comfortable and user-friendly. The response on campus

Above: Aerial view of commons.
Left: Garden Café.
Below left: Casual seating.
Below: Stair.
Opposite: Reference desk.
Photography: Dave Brown.

has been overwhelmingly positive. Doug Kaylor, the College's library Director, reports, "One word I hear students say again and again is 'awesome.'"

Champlin/Haupt Architects, Inc.

Northern Kentucky University
Power Plant & Parking Garage
Highland Heights, Kentucky

For college-bound students in greater Cincinnati, Northern Kentucky University is popular for its broad range of programs at the associate and bachelor degree levels, making it the region's second largest university. The main campus is also noted for its bland 70s-modern style concrete architecture, however, and the school has used two new developments, both designed by Champlin/Haupt Architects, to improve its campus image. Highlighted by a barrel-vaulted frontispiece housing boilers, the three-level Power Plant articulates its functions using bold, volumetric forms,

displaying equipment behind glass, and enclosing itself within a handsomely detailed façade. It could hardly do less, given its dramatic location atop a steep hillside. As for the three-level, 1,600 car parking garage, the University's desire for a new parking facility that is both vehicle and pedestrian friendly drove a design that appears effort-lessly functional – and yet unique to the campus. Not only is the lowest level set on-grade at the depressed elevation of the site's earlier soccer field, hiding its bulk from the campus, the front stairs occupy glass pavilions with glazed block-sheathed

elevator towers that promote safety and serve as destination points. Four lightwells divide the garage into five sections for phased construction. A pedestrian bridge links the structure to existing campus walkways, projecting an image so attractive it doubles as a campus gateway.

Right: Garage at dusk.

Bottom left: Garage pedestrian entrance.

Bottom right: Garage stairwell.

Opposite bottom left: Power plant exterior.

Opposite bottom right: Power plant interior.

Photography: David Steinbrunner, Greg Matulionis.

Champlin/Haupt Architects, Inc.

Wright State University
Boonshoft School of Medicine Expansion
Dayton, Ohio

How can new architectural forms and materials be sensitively integrated into an academic setting that has not deviated from an established, conservative aesthetic for decades? In Dayton, Ohio, an 18,000 square-foot addition to Fred White Center for Wright State University's Boonshoft School of Medicine, designed by Champlin/Haupt Architects, has brought modernity, discretion, and compassion into an academic lab setting. Through a new light-filled entry and state-of-the-art facilities such as a wireless, 160-seat tiered lecture room, three gross anatomy laboratories/classrooms and a full-functioning morgue, the school is able to offer medical students a first-rate education. Its design solutions display subtle innovations. The need to restrict indoor daylight is countered with a glazed corridor and entry tower. A new architectural vocabulary confronts an established aesthetic without overwhelming it by combining existing brick with limestone, phenolic panels, maple wood and other neutral materials, plus art walls, to quietly but decisively shift the visual focus. Varied architectural volumes achieve their complex forms with economical steel framing. Students are reminded of their Hippocratic Oath via the custom banners hung in the training center. For faculty and students of the School, families of the Anatomical Gift Donor Program, and the staff of the seven teaching hospitals in the Miami Valley served by the School's medical students, the new facility introduces a welcome modern design sensibility.

Top left: William A. Bernie Anatomy Learning & Surgical Training Center.

Top center: Faculty Office Corridor.

Top right: Entry Tower.

Left: 160-seat Ramesh K. and Saroj Gandhi Auditorium.

Photography: Dave Brown.

Cho Benn Holback + Associates

100 N. Charles Street
14th Floor
Baltimore, MD 21201
410.576.0440
410.332.8455 (Fax)
www.cbhassociates.com

Cho Benn Holback + Associates

Cho Benn Holback + Associates

University of Maryland, Baltimore County Public Policy Building
Baltimore, Maryland

Is there anything more timeless yet urgent than getting people from different walks of life to congregate, initiate dialogue and plan future cooperation? You can see this clearly in the development of the new, four-story, 62,000-square-foot Public Policy Building at the University of Maryland, Baltimore County. A public forum where academicians from different departments assemble for debates and discussions, designed by Cho Benn Holback + Associates, the facility occupies a prominent site on the University's 500-acre main campus, and includes a lecture hall, classrooms, meeting rooms and offices for six public policy-related academic departments, including Political Science, Public Policy, Economics, Sociology and Anthropology, Maryland Institute for Policy Analysis and Research, and Shriver Center. The design generates a strong outside-to-inside connection of public spaces with its exterior of brick, metal panels and glass, drawing people from the entry plaza into the two-story main lobby, which hosts public debates and lectures, the classrooms and conference rooms surrounding it, and beyond. Positioned to overlook the campus green space and define the northwest edge of a future academic quadrangle, and outfitted with warm, flexible interiors appointed in comfortable contemporary furnishings, it makes public and departmental interaction seem very compelling.

Top right: West façade.
Right: Stair in main lobby.
Below: Main Building entry.
Opposite top left: Main lobby.
Opposite top right: Lecture hall.
Photography: David Sundberg/ Esto.

Cho Benn Holback + Associates

Towson University
Johnny Unitas Stadium Field House and Sports Complex
Baltimore, Maryland

Good physical connections can unite a school's population in body and spirit, as successfully demonstrated by the Johnny Unitas Stadium Field House and Sports Complex, designed by Cho Benn Holback + Associates, at Baltimore's Towson University. The new, four-level, 50,000-square-foot structure rejoins the athletic department facilities with the stadium and extends a new, elliptical promenade between the new stadium seating bowl to the north and the existing seating and Field House to the south. Consequently, Towson sports now have locker rooms for three teams and visitors, sports facility and support, faculty and coachs' offices, general classrooms, and a large, multi-purpose assembly room. This combined program is all housed within a bold, modern exterior of brick, precast concrete, metal panels and glass that complements the stadium. Ironically, the project's greatest technical triumph may never be noticed on the 328-acre campus. The new construction has replaced the original stadium stands, which were slipping down a steep grade within the site's active stream valley, while tucking the Field House into the sloping terrain and terracing the levels to the field. That's plenty for the 140-year-old school's 18,000 students to cheer about—besides Tiger football, lacrosse, field hockey and track teams.

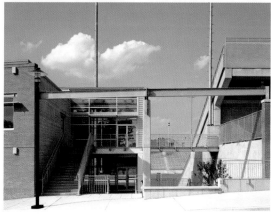

Top left: North Façade viewed from field.

Top right: South façade.

Above: Field house entry.

68

Above: Multi-purpose room.

Right: Entry corridor.

Photography: Kevin Chu/KCJP.

Cho Benn Holback + Associates

Messiah College
Larsen Student Union
Grantham, Pennsylvania

Poised between the academic and residential areas of Messiah College's 485-acre campus in Grantham, Pennsylvania, Larsen Student Union, a new, modern, two-floor, 30,000-square-foot building, designed by Cho Benn Holback + Associates, operates as a 24-hour amenity for the 97-year-old Christian liberal arts institution's 2,900 students. Can the design handle the job? Apparently, the brick, metal and glass structure, enclosing a double-height, multi-purpose space that serves as dining area and performance venue, a market-style servery with full-production kitchen, a gameroom, a campus radio station, and student club and government offices, is performing exactly as intended. The award-winning design's versatility is particularly evident in the multi-purpose space, where an open and accessible "coffee house" setting for touring bands replaces a campus basement. Here, the second floor seating rings the space, letting the whole building interact with performers, the glass curtain wall provides a colorful backdrop, the cantilevered roof offers a band shell for outdoor performances, and the sloping site supports a second floor entrance from student residences and a first floor entrance from the academic green. David Parkyn, Messiah's former senior vice president, asserts, "The success of this project is due in large part to the exceptional architectural team from Cho Benn Holback."

Below: Multi-purpose space.
Bottom left: Second floor lounge.
Bottom right: Fireside room.
Opposite top: South façade and lawn.
Opposite bottom: South entry plaza.
Photography: David Sundberg/Esto.

Cho Benn Holback + Associates

Baltimore School for the Arts
Baltimore, Maryland

Some of America's finest dance companies, orchestras, theaters and art galleries owe their artists to a remarkable public institution in Baltimore. Baltimore School for the Arts admits students based solely on auditions, and engages them in a rigorous college preparatory program—including pre-professional studies in visual arts, music, theatre and dance—that sends them to leading colleges and conservatories. To increase enrollment from 328 to 375, the school recently renovated and expanded its historic, seven-story home, the 1920 Alcazar Hotel, with a lively design by Cho Benn Holback + Associates. The 150,000-square-foot facility has been transformed by updating existing interiors, adding an adjacent historic brownstone and demolishing its non-original back wings to erect a new, three-story dance studio, enclosing the alley between the two structures as a connecting link, and replacing the main building's one-story core with a three-story addition. Such new accommodations as the library/media center, dance studios, music classrooms and practice rooms, theater studios and classrooms, scene shop, sculpture studio, and welding and kiln rooms, and such renovated ones as the auditorium, academic classrooms, science laboratories, painting and drawing studios, cafeteria, and faculty

and administrative offices, give departments greater cohesiveness while preserving the school's quirky, energetic spirit.

Top left: Bridge to new addition.
Top right: Entrance to addition.
Above: Dance studio.
Above right: Corridor.
Photography: Michael Dersin Photography.

72

Dagit • Saylor Architects

1100 Land Title Building
100 South Broad Street
Philadelphia, PA 19110
215.972.0500
215.972.8060 (Fax)
www.dagitsaylor.com

Dagit • Saylor Architects

Dagit • Saylor Architects

Lehigh University
Zoellner Performing Arts Center
Bethlehem, Pennsylvania

While the New York Philharmonic doesn't regularly perform on school stages, the inauguration of Lehigh University's 106,214-square-foot Zoellner Performing Arts Center, designed by Dagit • Saylor Architects, drew the orchestra under music director Kurt Mazur to the institution founded in 1865 by industrialist Asa Packer in Bethlehem, Pennsylvania. The Center continues to flourish by giving Lehigh's 6,641 students, 597 faculty members and residents of surrounding communities a highly versatile resource that includes the 1,000-seat Baker Hall for music, 350-seat Diamond Drama Hall, 125-seat black box theater, two-story art gallery, academic facilities for the departments of music and drama, support spaces and an attached, 345-car parking deck. Its design deftly acknowledges Lehigh's needs while enhancing community relations. Baker Hall, for example, becomes a 350-seat recital theater using a transondent curtain, the two main theaters sit back-to-back to share the scene shop, and the Center extends its activities outdoors through gardens and terraces. Being on the perimeter of Lehigh's 1,600-acre campus also lets the Center reach out to area residents as well as far-flung parts of the campus. Observes Augustine Ripa, chair of Lehigh's department of theater, "Our journey toward the Zoellner Arts Center was a best case scenario."

Cornell University
Appel Commons
Ithaca, New York

Midday at Appel Commons can be extremely busy though the new, 58,000-square-foot structure, designed by Dagit • Saylor Architects incorporating a 624-seat dining facility, lounge space, fitness center, retail, mail services and multi-program space, is not in the center of Cornell University's 750-acre campus in Ithaca, New York. The building helps anchor the new North Campus, where Cornell has located its entire 3,108-member freshman class, with an inviting community focus to support freshman life at the 141-year-old school. To connect all three levels and create a "see and be seen" ambience, major public spaces have clear views of one another, such as the dining facility's overview of the lobby lounge, interiors are visible from outside, particularly at night, and the building can be seen from the Central Campus. Also contributing to the milieu are the careful separation of service areas from public zones, the shifting of spaces within the orthogonal grid to resolve the site's multiple geometries, and the introduction of a marketplace dining experience with stylish individual cooking stations. "The place was just hopping at about 11:30 a.m.," declared Jean Reese, Cornell project leader, after a recent visit. "I wish I had a university photographer in tow!"

Top left: Mezzanine Stairway.
Left: Modular Meeting Rooms.
Below: Exterior.
Opposite: Servery.
Photography: Robert Barker, Cornell University Photographer.

Dagit • Saylor Architects

Pennsylvania Academy of the Fine Arts
Samuel M.V. Hamilton Building
Philadelphia, Pennsylvania

Above: Exterior.
Left: Sculpture Gallery.
Below left: Sculpture Study Center.
Bottom left: Painting Studio.
Opposite: Stair Hall.
Photography: Tom Crane Photography.

In an ironic twist, Philadelphia's famed Pennsylvania Academy of the Fine Arts has acquired and renovated the building across the street once criticized for blocking its natural light. The action benefits both the Academy's Landmark Building, an 1876 masterpiece designed by Frank Furness and George W. Hewitt for America's oldest art museum and school (1805), and its neighbor, an historic, 10-story, 300,000-square-foot former automobile showroom and parts storage facility designed in 1916 by Charles Oelschlager and transformed into the Samuel M.V. Hamilton Building through a design by Dagit • Saylor Architects. The Hamilton Building doubles gallery space and provides a consolidated administration area, café, gift shop, library and student services, several levels of sculpture, printmaking and foundry shops, individual student studios and major painting studios with northern light. Though the demolition of the historic first-floor interior was allowed by the Pennsylvania Historical and Museum Commission to give the Academy a first-floor temporary exhibition gallery, the building's exterior has been fully restored, and its upper floors have recaptured the loft-like character they displayed before offices filled them. As the Academy commented on its 200th anniversary, the Hamilton Building has strengthened the Academy's future by trading its display of automobiles for art.

Dagit • Saylor Architects

College of Wooster
Henry Luce III Residence Hall
Wooster, Ohio

If good fences make good neighbors, as Robert Frost so memorably asserted, the College of Wooster can take neighborly pride in its new, three-floor, 39,000-square-foot Henry Luce III Residence Hall, designed by Dagit • Saylor Architects for 96 students, located at the edge of its 240-acre campus in Wooster, Ohio. Luce Hall makes a graceful but unmistakable transition from the large houses of its surrounding residential neighborhood to the buildings on campus by subdividing its mass into three visually separate houses, adopting a residential-scale, five-part Georgian scheme consisting of a central pavilion, two flanking wings and connecting stair towers, all modeled in the Collegiate Gothic architecture of the 140-year-old school. The residence honors Wooster's desire for individualistic, smaller housing units by combining one- and two-story suites for six, nine or 12 students, singles and doubles with a formal lounge, meeting rooms, exercise room, language laboratory, computer room with desktop publishing capabilities, small library and seminar room. Not only does this arrangement give students more varied opportunities for lodging, it invites the campus to make active use of Luce Hall, integrating it with overall campus life. A sign of the dormitory's popularity among residents adorns a popular T-shirt: "Living Luce and Loving It!"

Upper left, clockwise: Bedroom, Living Room Overlook, Projecting Bay and Sunlit Corridor.

Top: Exterior.

Above: Lounge.

Photography: Tom Crane Photography.

Davis Brody Bond-Aedas

315 Hudson Street
New York, NY 10013
212.633.4700
212.633.4760 (Fax)
www.davisbrody.com

1025 33rd Street NW
Washington, DC 20007
202.449.1190
202.595.0509 (Fax)
info@davisbrody.com

Davis Brody Bond-Aedas

Davis Brody Bond-Aedas

Vanderbilt University
Eskind Biomedical Research Library
Nashville, Tennessee

Top left: Medical library stacks and reading tables.

Top right: Atrium.

Above: Exterior.

Opposite: Detail of curtainwall.

Photography: Paul Warchol.

How should libraries function in the Internet era? With librarians exploring the possibilities, one of the most ambitious new examples can be viewed at 133-year-old Vanderbilt University's new, award-winning Eskind Biomedical Research Library, in Nashville. The four-story, 80,000-square-foot medical library, incorporating the Center for Biomedical Informatics on the top floor, has been designed by Davis Brody Bond-Aedas as an integrated complex of print and electronic resources that doubles as a symbolic entrance to Vanderbilt's Medical Center. Its dramatic massing comprises a large block housing stacks and support spaces and a series of smaller volumes containing public spaces, all aligned with an east-west circulation spine and enclosed in precast concrete and glass. Among the features that make it particularly effective are a convertible stack zone, half of which can yield to electronic workstations and collaborative work spaces, a fourth floor of flexible work stations and demonstration areas, a versatile meeting room for the Medical Center Board with catering facilities, and interior appointments combining traditional materials and comfortable furnishings to sustain the warm, scholarly atmosphere of a traditional library. Reports former library director T. Mark Hodges, "The building exceeds our expectations, and it has been well accepted and praised by all."

Davis Brody Bond-Aedas

University of Connecticut
Pharmacy/Biology Building
Storrs, Connecticut

Academic gatherings take on multiple meanings at the University of Connecticut's new Pharmacy/Biology Building on its Storrs campus. The 220,000-square-foot facility, designed by Davis Brody Bond-Aedas as a six-story laboratory building and six-story block of academic space and faculty offices, fosters collaboration among the University's biological and pharmaceutical scientists through state-of-the-art teaching and research laboratories, vivarium, NMR facility, library/learning center, faculty and administrative offices, two 120-seat lecture halls (one with fixed seating on a sloped floor, one dividable with stackable seating on a flat floor), student lounge, and two atriums. In addition, it restores the proximity that all three biology departments in the College of Liberal Arts and Sciences, namely physiology, neurobiology, and molecular and cell biology, last enjoyed on campus over a decade ago. Finally, the design reverses a decision made in the 1950s that housed the pharmacy and biology departments in concrete and brick-clad boxes with dark and dreary spaces by laying out spacious interiors with plenty of natural light, including lecture halls, teaching laboratories, student lounge and student lockers, areas that traditionally had no natural light whatsoever. Scientists accustomed to the encumbrances of the past are delighted that the new space has set them free.

Above: Aerial view of exterior.

Far left: Entry atrium.

Left: Lecture room.

Opposite: Exterior as seen in quadrangle.

Photography: Neil Alexander.

Davis Brody Bond-Aedas

Dillard University
DUICEF Building
New Orleans, Louisiana

Top left: Entrance.
Top right: Evening view of exterior.
Right: Study Lounge.
Opposite: Atrium.
Photography: Neil Alexander.

Picture an appropriate image for the first new building in a decade on the New Orleans campus of Dillard University, a private, historically black, liberal arts institution founded in 1869. For Davis Brody Bond-Aedas, designing the two-story, 30,000-square-foot Dillard University Inter-national Center for Economic Freedom (DUICEF) required diligence and flexibility as well as creativity. Since the new facility would stand near the north end of campus beside the London Canal, one of New Orleans's drainage channels, with specimen oak trees on site to be saved and Kabacoff Quadrangle located due west, its massing became long, narrow and angled. To relate to neighboring white neoclassical buildings on campus while acknowledging the importance of change and growth for the University, its architecture evolved into an elegant expression of Modernism. Inside, the frequently busy DUICEF reflects the importance of teacher education to Dillard by offering five multi-purpose classrooms, three specialized teaching laboratories, three conference spaces, a lecture hall, a study lounge and 15 student work stations. These spaces partly encircle a naturally lighted, two-story lobby and result in a bright, open environment that contrasts dramatically with older campus interiors, giving Dillard a facility that glows visually and symbolically as a beacon on campus.

Davis Brody Bond-Aedas

King/Robinson Magnet School
New Haven, Connecticut

Top left: Exterior in landscape.
Top right: Circulation spine.
Far left: Courtyard.
Left: Gymnasium.
Photography: Elliott Kaufman.

Nobody was sorry to see the old, brutalist school building demolished. In fact, the King/Robinson Magnet School, one of New Haven Public Schools' newest Magnet Schools, designed by Davis Brody Bond-Aedas, accommodates the neighborhood and academic community in ways its predecessor never could. Its three-story, 102,000-square-foot brick and glass-clad structure serves 650 K-8 students with a comprehensive building program, including an interior atrium, library/media/conference center, art room, science classrooms and prep rooms, music instructional rooms, special education/language laboratory, computer training facility, gymnasium/community space, cafeteria, kitchen, orchestra room and stage, offices, conference areas, lounges and guidance suites. Paradoxically, the building feels intimate despite its inevitable bulk. Whereas the old school dominated the center of its site, King/Robinson tucks into a hillside to reduce its visibility to residents. Students, faculty and staff find interiors easy to navigate, thanks to a scheme that features courtyards as "village squares," corridors that act as "streets," classrooms that occupy a "bar/loft" zone flexible enough to accommodate almost any teaching method, and a carefully conceived site orientation that turns the school into a "sundial" as sunlight traverses its entire length. The result is a successful school where even the building earns A's. Awards, that is.

EHDD

500 Treat Avenue
Suite 201
San Francisco, CA 94110
415.285.9193
415.285.3866 (Fax)
www.EHDD.com

EHDD

Valparaiso University
Christopher Center for Library and Information Resources
Valparaiso, Indiana

Is this a library? The new, four-level, 108,000-square-foot Christopher Center for Library and Information Resources at Valparaiso University, in Valparaiso, Indiana, designed by EHDD, not only functions as a main campus library with automated storage retrieval for low-use book storage. It also houses a 250- to 300-seat multi-purpose community room with catering kitchen, executive board room, training rooms, sloped floor classrooms, collaborative computer laboratory, faculty lounge, casual reading and group study areas, café, and student lounges with fireplaces, all sustained by a user-friendly environment. Nevertheless, the Center projects an understated image on the 310-acre campus of this respected, liberal arts institution founded in 1859. The modern brick, concrete and glass structure defers to Resurrection Chapel and other campus buildings, acknowledges its sloping site by minimizing its height, connects with an existing student union where it will eventually expand, and maximizes daylight while minimizing glare through generous windows and a monumental sunscreen. But its interior is truly breathtaking. To quote Richard AmRhein, Valparaiso's dean of library services, "The challenge these days is engaging people in the building. So we made it much more than a hushed research collection." He notes that students, books, cappuccino and conversation co-exist here perfectly.

Above: Exterior with sunscreen.

Right: Collaborative computer laboratory.

Far right: Library.

Opposite top: Community room.

Opposite bottom left: Student lounge.

Opposite bottom right: Sloped floor classroom.

Photography: Peter Aaron/ Esto Photographics.

EHDD

University of California, Berkeley
Residence Halls, Units I and II, Infill Student Housing
Berkeley, California

Room and board are major undertakings at University of California, Berkeley, which houses 10,400 of "Cal's" 23,482 undergraduate and 10,076 graduate students on its 1,232-acre campus. In an award-winning project adding 884 beds on 267,500 square feet (including 50,000 square feet of renovated space) in four new, seven-story freestanding buildings and two existing buildings, EHDD designed dormitory and apartment-style residence halls as infill housing. This increases housing density, improves the quality of life for residents and softens the impact of existing nine-story residence halls on the

neighborhood. The facilities are extensive, including such student services spaces as computer lounges, tutoring center, music practice, fitness center, group study lounges and conference rooms, in addition to dwelling units in slab structures that step down from seven stories to four. Yet the concrete, metal panel and glass-sheathed structures mitigate their bulk through massing, color and architectural detailing, reinforcing the streetscape on one side with shallow front yards and entry porches, and introducing a central patio above student services on the other side. (The old central dining facility

demolished for the patio has been replaced by Crossroads dining commons.) As for the loft-style apartments, they wow everyone who sees them at the 138-year-old school.

Top left: Student lounge.
Top right: Student apartment.
Above: Aerial view of extrior.
Opposite: Exterior elevation.
Photography: Peter Aaron/ Esto Photographics, Proehl tudios© (aerial shot)

EHDD

Carnegie Institution of Washington
Global Ecology Research Center
Stanford, California

In 2001, after 70-plus years, the Carnegie Institution of Washington chose Stanford University as the site of its newest scientific research center, the Department of Global Ecology. The opening of the new, two-floor, 10,900-square-foot Global Ecology Research Center, designed by EHDD, formally establishes the Department on the west side of Stanford's 8,180-acre campus. This low-key yet innovative building is a fitting home for the Department, which conducts basic research on the interactions between the earth's ecosystems, land, atmosphere and oceans. It simultaneously maximizes energy efficiency, minimizes waste and incorporates recycled materials in a flexible facility where daylight and natural ventilation serve a laboratory with movable benches and shelves, reconfigurable private and open offices, conference room, meeting rooms and indoor/outdoor lobby. Though its design embodies many well-known environmental methodologies, the architect was encouraged to bypass LEED's diffused focus and drastically reduce carbon impact while meeting the highest standards of comfort and performance—reducing carbon emissions associated with the building's materials and operations by over 80

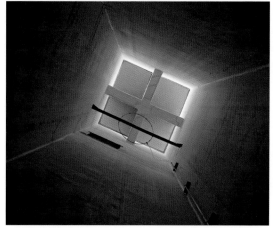

percent—while pursuing habitat and water conservation goals. Is the construction meeting its operational goals? A post-occupancy study by the Center for the

Built Environment placed it second out of 158 buildings studied for occupational satisfaction.

Top: Exterior.

Above left: Cooling tower.

Above right: Laboratory.

Opposite: Corridor and private office.

Photography: Peter Aaron/ Esto Photographics.

EHDD

University of Cincinnati
Sawyer Hall
Cincinnati, Ohio

A progressive institution since its founding in 1819, the University of Cincinnati, in Cincinnati, Ohio, is working with EHDD to transform Sawyer Hall, a 1960s high-rise dormitory, into a virtually all-new, 450-bed, 13-floor, 150,000-square-foot student residence. Stripping the building to its structure, the project will install contemporary student apartments along double-loaded corridors atop a first level holding a series of public spaces that will create an active ground level perimeter. A new student services building, placed between Sawyer Hall and an adjacent tower, will feature two large public spaces boldly cantilevered over an entry lobby. The most significant design problem in transforming the student residence, however, has been to design a new skin that can deal with the seasonal temperature extremes of the Midwest and the building's east-west exposures to reduce energy consumption enough to meet LEED Silver requirements. The solution is a super-insulated skin employing a double-wall system of metal panels, brick and glass to provide R-25 insulation and reduce solar gain through glazing having a shading coefficient of 0.34. Still, for the school that gave the world such firsts as antihistamine, cooperative education and the electronic organ, Sawyer Hall is just another day's breakthrough.

Top left: South Elevation.
Top right: Full exterior view.
Above: Close up of entrance.
Illustration: Courtesy of EHDD.

FXFOWLE ARCHITECTS, PC

22 West 19 Street
New York, NY 10011
212.627.1700
212.463.8716 (Fax)
info@fxfowle.com
www.fxfowle.com

FXFOWLE ARCHITECTS, PC

Syracuse University
Martin J. Whitman School of Management
Syracuse, New York

In a bold move to fulfill the potential of its business programs, enhance competitive position, and plant a campus gateway on a prominent downtown site, Syracuse University in Syracuse, New York, recently opened a new, 165,000-square-foot home for its Martin J. Whitman School of Management for 1,400 undergraduate and graduate students and distance learners. The building responds to surroundings as well as occupants with a modernist aesthetic in brick, metal and glass that acknowledges a nearby 11-story hotel, various low- and mid-rise commercial and University structures, fraternity houses and a parking garage. Its internal functions are articulated as separate volumes with distinctive forms and links to a multi-level internal circulation "street." To dramatize their importance, its 22 classrooms are clustered in a three/four-story element recessed from the street and framed like a jewelry box between the hotel and the building's masonry components, adjacent to the building's focal point, a three-story, 4,000-square-foot glass atrium. With such additional facilities as an auditorium, meeting rooms, student lounges and computer clusters, café, and faculty and administrative offices, the school draws compliments to Syracuse University, which *U.S. News & World Report* calls one of America's top 50 undergraduate business programs.

Top left: Detail of staircase.
Top right: Exterior at dusk.
Above: Tiered classroom.
Right: Building detail.
Opposite: Atrium.
Photography: Jeff Goldberg/ESTO.

FXFOWLE ARCHITECTS, PC

The New School
Arnhold Hall, Theresa Lang Cultural Center
New York, New York

It's the rare New Yorker who encounters buildings without multiple identities in a city settled in 1625. Consider The New School, which recently converted a former 19th-century department store into Arnhold Hall, an academic facility housing the splendid new Theresa Lang Cultural Center. The legendary, progressive university, founded in 1919 by historian Charles Beard, philosopher John Dewey, and economists Thorstein Veblen and James Harvey Robinson, operated in the 1920s using six rented brownstones. Yet there's nothing outdated about the design of Lang Center. Encompassing the first two floors of Arnhold Hall, the facility offers flexible, multi-purpose spaces for large and small lectures, receptions, entertainment, executive dining, pre-function events, and exhibits in an environment blending Modern design with such historic elements as cast-iron columns. The installation proclaims its importance to the campus through a dynamic combination of architecture and art. Not only is its lobby anchored by a distinctive illuminated staircase and a bold mural by renowned artist Sol LeWitt that stretches from the front door to the second floor, there are works by other influential contemporary artists to keep the building and its occupants focused on achieving progress in the 21st century and beyond.

Top left: Meeting room.
Top right: Staircase.
Above left: Lecture hall.
Above: Gallery/Multi-purpose space.
Photography: David Sunberg/ ESTO.

FXFOWLE ARCHITECTS, PC

The Calhoun School
New York, New York

Who says a 110-year-old progressive, independent, college preparatory school located in Manhattan's West Side is too old to grow? That's what the Calhoun School convincingly declares with its new, 30,500-square-foot renovation and expansion. Calhoun houses 670 boys and girls ranging from three-year-olds to twelfth graders in two locations less than a mile apart, with students in grades 2-12 occupying the main building, a five-story concrete and travertine structure originally built in 1974. After a com-prehensive master plan and feasibility study, the school decided to create more program space in the building by adding four stories, a mezzanine level and a green roof, in addition to com-pletely remaking the existing space. The results have been dramatic, giving the school a two-story performing arts center with a 234-seat black box theater as the centerpiece. Surrounded by rehearsal spaces, a set design shop and music instructional spaces, the three-quarter round theater provides flex-ible performance space for the arts department and spe-cialized teaching space for all the arts. A 5,200-square-foot gymnasium stands at the top floor of the addition, flooding its space with daylight from clerestory windows and mak-ing Calhoun look quite fit for a centenarian.

Top left: Black box theater.
Top right: Gymnasiam.
Above right: Laboratory.
Left: Exterior.
Photography: James D'Addio.

101

FXFOWLE ARCHITECTS, PC

The Spence School
New York, New York

With grade schools increasingly developing separate, specialized facilities for different age groups, the Spence School, an independent college-preparatory day school for girls in grades K-12, founded in 1892 on Manhattan's Upper East Side, recently relocated its Lower School to a newly acquired building. Happily, all 600 Spence students benefited. Not only did Lower School students acquire a warm, friendly and child-centered environment, remaining Middle and Upper School students found fresh educational opportunities as well. In integrating the 20,000-square-feet vacated by the Lower School in a more spacious and modern academic setting, FXFOWLE developed and carried out a master plan for the renovation of the entire original, nine-story building—the work of Beaux Arts architect John Russell Pope—that created a distinctive Middle School identity. Strategically locating the Middle School on floors 8 and 9, and inserting special purpose and administrative spaces between the two schools, the plan clarified circulation and established a new Middle School commons area and 11 new classrooms to provide needed flexibility. Additional facilities, including more classrooms, black box theater and art rooms, emerged from occupied areas during the summer to minimize disturbance and give Middle and Upper School students a memorable back-to-school surprise.

FXFOWLE ARCHITECTS, PC

The Juilliard School
New York, New York

Right: Main lobby.
Bottom right: Entrance.

New York's world-renowned Lincoln Center, one of America's oldest and most respected urban forums for the performing arts, is getting a facelift—a respectful operation that will complement the existing architecture and public spaces while it revitalizes the public experience. Among the anticipated interventions, the extension of The Juilliard School, a leading American conservatory and a key component of Lincoln Center, calls for the main lobby to be framed by a soaring, glass-enclosed entrance making the school more accessible and visible at street level. To help maintain the school's artistic excellence, all of the building's performance-related spaces will also be acoustically isolated from neighboring spaces and outfitted with advanced technology and equipment. Extensive additions and new facilities will include new teaching studios, practice rooms, dance rehearsal rooms, black box theater, general-purpose classrooms, and faculty and administrative offices. In addition, the lobby of Alice Tully Hall, the home of the Juilliard Orchestra, Juilliard Symphony, and Chamber Music Society of Lincoln Center, will be updated to give it a street presence. This project is designed in association with Diller Scofidio + Renfro.

FXFOWLE ARCHITECTS, PC

Perth Amboy High School
Perth Amboy, New Jersey

This finalist entry for a new Perth Amboy High School competition aims to establish an environment where the cultural multiplicity of a blighted industrial city is encouraged, and a robust stage is built for coherent, participatory education. The design solution, gives form to the school's educational vision by housing its five academies in discrete, permeable units dispersed across the site. From the relatively open classrooms to the generous public spaces, students can observe campus activities and be seen by classmates, promoting self-awareness and overall consciousness of the entire school community. To enable the school to serve as both an integrated sustainable network and environmental teaching tool, the design offers such progressive features as a green roof, natural ventilation, active management of storm water runoff, structural insulated panels, and ample natural lighting. Equally important, the design is zoned so the school can be readily shared by local residents and the academic community. While the public spends time in the area closest to the active boulevard, buses carrying students arrive at a more internalized entrance in the quieter, academically focused western sector, letting the two groups happily co-exist.

Top: Academic core.
Above: Courtyard.
Right: Student lobby.

Glavé & Holmes Associates

801 East Main Street
Suite 300
Richmond, VA 23219
804.649.9303
804.343.3378 (Fax)
www.glaveandholmes.com
marketing@glaveandholmes.com

Glavé & Holmes Associates

Glavé & Holmes Associates

Union Theological Seminary and Presbyterian School of Christian Education
William Smith Morton Library
Richmond, Virginia

Above: Atrium ceiling.
Left: Exterior.
Bottom left: Reserve reading room.
Opposite: Atrium.
Photography: Maxwell MacKenzie.

Responding to society's needs since 1812, Union Theological Seminary and Presbyterian School of Christian Education, in Richmond, Virginia, has provided education for the Christian ministry within the Reformed tradition of the Presbyterian Church that is "scholarly, pastoral, and engaged with contemporary life." An eloquent example of its pragmatism is William Smith Morton Library, a four-level, 68,000-square-foot facility, designed by Glavé & Holmes Associates. Although the Seminary preserves the historic character

of Schauffler Hall, the 1919 chapel it transformed into Morton Library, it has made needed changes to create a state-of-the-art information center. To accommodate the new library, with it's research center, reserved reading room, reference library, climate-controlled archival facility and support spaces, the exisiting building has metamorphosed into a larger structure encircling a light-filled atrium naturally lit by groin-vaulted louvers, with concrete flooring replacing wood floors to gain load bearing capacity. The historic front façade was

preserved and the original west wall incorporated into a contemporary interior enriched with appropriate iconography. The William Smith Morton Library's superiority over it's predecessor is demonstrated regularly by students who come more often and stay longer. Notes associate librarian Robert Benedetto, "People tell us how much they enjoy the library."

Glavé & Holmes Associates

Randolph-Macon College
Thomas Branch Hall
Ashland, Virginia

Placing an atrium at the center of a dormitory might seem counterintuitive for student residents given the potential for distraction. However, that's not the case at Randolph-Macon College's newly renovated and expanded Thomas Branch Hall. Keeping up with the times comes naturally for Randolph-Macon, which began in 1830 as a school for prospective clergymen of the Methodist Church and evolved into a Methodist-af-

filiated college of the liberal arts and sciences serving some 1,118 students of all faiths on its 116-acre campus in Ashland, Virginia. What prompted the makeover of three-story, 25,300-square-foot Branch Hall, designed by Glavé & Holmes Associates, was the school's desire to combine existing accommodations for private residential life with new elements supporting student social and academic life. The new scheme places the College's Peaks of Excellence Center, computer laboratory, seminar spaces, staff counseling and other offices on the ground floor, and locates undergraduate residences on the upper floors, lining the atrium with student "living rooms" where students can informally gather and interact. With careful sound insulation and warm, modern interiors of slate, carpet, linoleum, cherry wood trim and comfortable, contemporary furnishings, Branch Hall has performed so well it has become the standard for future student housing projects.

Top left: Exterior.
Top right: Staircase.
Above: Lounge.
Opposite: Atrium.
Photography: Regi Franz and Thomas Kojcsich.

Glavé & Holmes Associates

University of Virginia
Peabody Hall
Charlottesville, Virginia

When prospective students and their families arrive at Peabody Hall, the University of Virginia's Office of Admission, expecting to see evidence of the venerable institution founded in Charlottesville by Thomas Jefferson in 1819, they're not disappointed. What they probably don't realize, however, is that this 1920s classroom building lost most of its original interiors to earlier remodeling. Thanks to a thoughtful renovation designed by Glavé & Holmes Associates, the three-level, 23,330-square-foot space nevertheless offers an inviting and convincing reception for visitors as well as functional space for the Office of Admission. The new offices, reception areas, meeting rooms and support facilities respond directly to Admission's programming needs while combining existing "clues" with period-style architecture and furnishings to create a visual language for the interiors. Numerous techniques have been devised to enrich the experience for visitors. Naturally lighted areas are maximized, for example, by moving "non-person" functions such as file storage away from them, primary mechanical equipment is concentrated in hallways to free habitable spaces for taller ceilings, a T-shaped entry hall simplifies circulation, and high technology services are discreetly integrated with architectural detailing for easy access. Why shouldn't Mr. Jefferson's community of scholars greet visitors with a bright, classical face?

Above: Reception desk.
Top left: Entry lobby.
Right: Corridor.
Opposite: Central hall.
Photography: Robert Chancler.

Glavé & Holmes Associates

University of Virginia, Darden School of Business Administration Sponsors' Hall and Parking Deck
Charlottesville, Virginia

A casual stroll through the grounds of the University of Virginia's Darden School of Business Administration could leave many a visitor convinced that Thomas Jefferson, who founded the University and designed the revered Academical Village (1822-1826) at the heart of the Charlottesville campus, touched Darden's Palladian-style buildings as well. However, the Darden School was founded in 1954, and its elegant facilities are scarcely a decade old. Not surprisingly, the University asked that the new, 500-car, four-level, 152,890-square-foot parking garage and two- and four-story, 47,585-square-foot Sponsor's Hall addition, designed by Glavé & Holmes Associates in association with Ayers Saint Gross Architects, "be sensitively integrated with existing campus structures." Sponsor's Hall, Darden's executive

education residence hotel, reprises Jefferson's concept of linked pavilions by stepping its units up the sloping site, creating a new, tripartite building with a central entry at the top of the hill. To produce a harmonious parking deck, an arcaded façade anchored by two stair towers serves as its primary elevation, tucking two levels into the hillside to reduce its visibility. Mark Reisler, the University's Associate Dean for Administration, reports, "Glavé & Holmes enthusiasm for working with the Darden School as a client was evident at all levels of the project."

Top left: Stair tower for parking deck.

Top right: Overhead view of Parking deck.

Above: Entrance to Sponsor's Hall.

Photography: Glavé & Holmes Associates.

112

Gwathmey Siegel & Associates Architects, llc

475 Tenth Avenue
3rd Floor
New York, NY 10018
212.947.1240
212.967.0890 (Fax)
www.gwathmey-siegel.com

Gwathmey Siegel & Associates Architects, llc

University of Cincinnati
Tangeman University Center
Cincinnati, Ohio

Above: Exterior seen from MainStreet.

Right: Addition to exterior.

Bottom right: Dining area overlooking Sports Stadium.

Opposite: Atrium.

Photography: Brad Feinknopf.

As the source of such inventions as the first antihistamine, first safe anti-knock gasoline, and first cooperative education program in America, the University of Cincinnati, founded in 1819, has never been shy about exposing its 35,244 students and 5,348 faculty members to real world experience. The development of MainStreet, a contemporary district serving students' academic and social interests, shows the school is equally pragmatic about using modern design on its historic, 473-acre campus. In fact, a linchpin of MainStreet, the recently reopened Tangeman University Center, designed by Gwathmey Siegel & Associates, boldly blends past and present. Enhancing Tangeman as a campus hub where students can "see and be seen," the design for the seven-story, 180,000-square-foot structure preserves the original 1935 Georgian building's façade, roof and tower; cuts out floors and reveals structure to create a three-story, skylit atrium; and surrounds it with a sleek zinc-and-glass-sheathed addition. The dynamic environment includes a foodcourt/dining area, cyber lounge, 200-seat movie theater, game room, campus bookstore and café, great hall, flexible meeting rooms, atrium/casual seating area, and new outdoor plaza connection to adjacent Nippert Stadium. Students are so pleased with the results that the foodcourt ran out of food during its first two days.

Gwathmey Siegel & Associates Architects, llc

Middlebury College
Middlebury College Library
Middlebury, Vermont

So many books and no cappuccino? Though cafes aren't mandated in libraries, progressive institutions such as Middlebury College, a liberal arts institution founded in 1800 in Middlebury, Vermont, regularly stay abreast of technological and cultural trends. For the new, three-level, 143,000-square-foot Middlebury College Library, designed by Gwathmey Siegel & Associates, the school has focused on expanding room for collections, increasing seating for the growing student body, and providing distinctive environ-ments for collaborative learning supported by the latest technology infrastructure. The building, which is open to residents of the nearby town, also demonstrates the college's continuing commitment to green design. Ample seating in group study and meeting rooms supports increasingly popular interactive and collaborative learning. And the interiors of the granite, limestone and marble structure (the building materials of the historic campus) are light-filled and offer generous views of the countryside. Thus, reading rooms occupy the upper level at the east and west ends, while the main level houses the circulation and reference desks, media rooms and laboratories, web seminar rooms, and 24-hour café. Periodicals, technical rooms, offices and special collections stacks are on the lower level, with library stacks occupying central positions on all three levels, flanked by classrooms and seating areas, in this splendid gateway into the 21st century.

Above: Atrium.

Left: Entry.

Opposite top: Exterior from Academic Green.

Opposite far left: East reading room.

Opposite left: Third floor stacks and carrels.

Photography: Scott Frances/ ESTO.

Gwathmey Siegel & Associates Architects, llc

Lawrence Technological University
University Technology and Learning Complex
Southfield, Michigan

Esteemed for grooming leaders in engineering, architecture, design and management, Lawrence Technological University, in Southfield, Michigan, has shown it is equally savvy in the design and functioning of the man-made world. Realizing that an upgraded architectural image could increase its competitiveness with neighboring schools, instill a growing residential student population with a genuine sense of place, and produce a more coherent physical environment, the University has developed the new, four-story, 135,000-square-foot University Technology and Learning Complex, designed by Gwathmey Siegel & Associates, as a state-of-the-art academic building and monumental "front door" to its 125-acre campus. The Complex achieves its goals with economy and style. Its coolly modern, linear structure houses fully-wired classrooms, virtual reality laboratory, advanced graphics laboratory, lighting laboratory, electrical engineering and computer laboratories. It also offers a photography studio, TV production and broadcasting studios for long-distance learning, galleries, lecture rooms, resource center and 15,000-volume library, conference room and office space. Wrapped in ribbed steel panels, ceramic tile, zinc shingles and glass, it features a three-story, covered portal leading to its interior and the campus. Visitors entering the sweeping, two-story ground-floor lobby and its lively information commons know exactly where they've arrived.

Gwathmey Siegel & Associates Architects, llc

New Jersey Institute of Technology
Campus Center and Academic Building
Newark, New Jersey

Students at New Jersey Institute of Technology know the respected public university is light years and just steps from its origin in 1884 as Newark Technical School. Created to train technicians for industry, the Institute simultaneously offers students undergraduate and graduate programs, and conducts cutting-edge research, often in partnership with industry. But it remains surrounded by a low-income residential neighborhood that shapes its destiny to this day. Thus, when Gwathmey Siegel & Associates designed the new three-story Campus Center and seven-story Academic Building, a 371,000-square-foot renovation and addition, it addressed such issues as a poorly defined sense of place, a need for a safe, welcoming refuge where a growing student body could study, relax and eat, and a shortage of office and classroom space. The new facilities are visibly improving campus life. Not only does the Campus Center wrap an addition around the existing building to double its size and provide such timely amenities as an attractive cafeteria, game rooms, faculty dining, pub, ballroom, meeting room and student offices. It links directly into the new Academic Building's offices, classrooms and conference areas via a new, third-floor pedestrian bridge, and projects an expansive, upbeat view of life on the 45-acre campus.

Right: View from Academic Building to Campus Center.

Below: Academic Building with pedestrian bridge.

Bottom: Aerial view showing green roof and solar panels.

Photography: James D'Addio.

H + L Architecture

1621 18th Street
Suite 110
Denver, CO 80202
303.295.1792
303.292.6437 (Fax)
www.hlarch.com

219 East Colorado Avenue
Colorado Springs, CO 80903
719.578.9317
719.578.9548 (Fax)

H + L Architecture

H + L Architecture

Erie High School
Erie, Colorado

Above: Exterior at main entrance.
Far right: Landscaping/plaza.
Right: Student forum.
Opposite: Commons.
Photography: Jeff Scroggins.

To experience the vitality public schools can contribute to everyday life, join some of the 12,000 residents of Erie, Colorado, a fast growing community 23 miles northwest of Denver, at recently completed Erie High School. Erie High is a two-story, 160,000-square-foot facility on a 61-acre campus, designed by H + L Architecture to serve the community as well as 1,200 students in grades 9-12. Its dual focus is typical of a town proud to be "off the beaten path." From its distinctive architecture, a modern abstraction in masonry, wood and steel of the region's historic coal mines meant to capture a "spirit of place," to specific accommodations for class-rooms, administration, media center, 600-seat auditorium, performing arts, visual arts, athletics and student commons, the school actively supports its constituents. It's a "school within a school," giving centrally located class-room "neighborhoods" easy access to specialized facilities and student commons so students can avail them-selves of extra help or added enrichment. It's a community resource during off-hours that gives Erie residents a personal stake in their high school. Pleased that students and faculty helped plan the replacement for the original 1929 high school, principal Steve Payne observes, "The students are so proud of the building."

122

H + L Architecture

Pioneer Ridge Elementary School
Johnstown, Colorado

"Small town USA" is a potent American vision of the good life that gives the 477 K-5 students of Pioneer Ridge Elementary School, in Johnstown, Colorado, a sense that they are all special and cherished. In fact, the new, one-story, 52,000-square-foot facility, designed by H + L Architecture, successfully blends the findings of a study on the area's agricultural history with the best qualities of a close-knit community to create a prototypical space for functionality and efficiency. Within a building resembling a cluster of individual buildings illuminated by classic old street lamps, a "main street" links Pioneer Ridge's classroom neighborhoods to the core services of administration, gymnasium and student commons, while a "town square" area supports group learning through educational lounges with carpeted seating ledges that drop below floor level. Other spaces, including dedicated areas for administration, media center, visual arts and music, help reinforce the scheme by reprising the vocabulary of concrete masonry, metal panels, curtain wall glazing in agrarian colors. Rick Baldino, principal of Pioneer Ridge, happily reports, "The kids love being here, especially on the playground and town squares. Our attendance and parental participation are up. And when kids are happy they focus on learning."

Top right: Classroom.

Above right: Class in neighborhood commons.

Right: Exterior at main entry.

Opposite: Neighborhood commons.

Photography: Jeff Scroggins.

124

H + L Architecture

University of Denver
Frank H. Ricketson Jr. Law Building
Denver, Colorado

Top left: Exterior.
Top right: Caseroom.
Above right: Library.
Above: Entry forum.
Opposite: Lobby
Photography: Jim Berchert.

Just 28 years after Colorado territorial governor John Evans established the University of Denver in 1864, the College of Law opened its doors. Accordingly the new, six-level, 242,860 square foot building designed by H + L Architecture in association with Shepley Bulfinch Richardson and Abbott and the office of the University Architect, Mark Rodgers, AIA, celebrates its heritage with a modern interpretation of Tuscan architecture in brick and limestone. The building, designed to house the Sturm College of Law, features the University of Denver's signature tower capped by a 48-foot copper spire and roof. The architecture's respect for the past is balanced by the interior's focus on the present and future. The award-winning design, encompassing classrooms, 120-seat lecture hall, law library and technology center for legal research, conferencing facilities, moot courtrooms, offices, cafeteria, and underground and structured parking, addresses such timely concerns as flexibility, environmental design and technology integration. Accordingly, the library spreads across three floors to facilitate interaction with other school facilities, students, faculty and staff. They are encouraged to meet through a spacious, two-story "forum" connected to the main entry, library entry and food service entry, and open space, natural light and Internet connections that flourish everywhere. Having met its goals so decisively, the University has declared, "We hired the best architects we could find."

H + L Architecture

University of Colorado at Colorado Springs University Center
Colorado Springs, Colorado

Below: Café.
Bottom left: Exterior.
Below right: Stair.
Bottom right: Entertainment area.
Photography: Jim Berchert.

One of Colorado's fastest growing universities, the University of Colorado at Colorado Springs, one of three campuses in the University of Colorado system, recently did what any growing family would do when its 7,800 students and faculty and staff members needed more space in the University Center, its campus community center. It remodeled and expanded the existing structure, producing a facility of 90,300 square feet on three floors to house such activities as student government and other student organizations, meeting rooms, pub/game room, food services, lounges, fitness center, bookstore and convenience store. Better yet, the reinvigorated Center, designed by H + L Architecture in association with Shepley Bulfinch Richardson & Abbott, introduces a glass-sheathed "link" to join three existing buildings in a coherent ensemble with one identifiable entry point, stretching from the first level of the adjacent library building to the Center complex. Long-established paths of pedestrian travel across an outdoor rooftop plaza engaged by the connecting link remain uninterrupted, with the addition's transparency maintaining cross-campus views and encouraging pedestrian passage. Tom Ostenberg, UCCS's director of facilities services, recently said of the design team, "I am particularly impressed with your ability to collaboratively work with the members of the University."

HMC Architects

3270 Inland Empire Blvd.
Ontario, CA 91764-4854
909.989.9979
909.483.1400 (Fax)
www.hmcarchitects.com

HMC Architects

Santee Education Complex
Los Angeles, California

Accommodating 877,010 students (2004 – 2005) in the nation's second largest public school system is no small task; nonetheless the Los Angeles Unified School District (LAUSD) is succeeding. Designed by HMC Architects, the Santee Education Complex is the first high school to open as part of LAUSD's $19.2 billion construction and repair program to build more than 150 new schools by 2012. The program received the Urban Land Institute's 2006 Award for Excellence. Santee is an award-winning, one- to three-story, 252,270-SF facility for 2,199 students that turns a commercial and industrial zone of south Los Angeles into an open and welcoming environment. Santee anchors its new environment on numerous levels. It borders a residential area, emphasizes small learning communities, and establishes a much-needed neighborhood landmark. The classrooms, library, gymnasium, auditorium, stadium, pool, administrative facilities, baseball field, softball field, hard courts, and underground parking occupy a main classroom building. Ancillary structures border an open courtyard. A landscaped arroyo at the center of campus is surrounded by a perimeter wall. Responding to site conditions, the playing fields and grass areas are oriented to the south-facing residential neighborhood, while the multistory buildings are clustered beside the north-facing commercial and industrial zone. By contrast, the cheerful yellow exterior honors a universal icon, the No. 2 pencil.

Top left: Exterior detail.
Top right: Library.
Above: Auditorium.
Right: Aerial view.
Opposite right: Courtyard view of exterior.
Photography: Claudia Ambriz, Ryan Beck, and Warren Aerial Photography, Inc.

HMC Architects

Solana Pacific Elementary School
San Diego, California

Solana Pacific Elementary School's innovative, civic-minded learning environment captures the eye and imagination of adults and children alike in Carmel Valley, a community within greater San Diego. Designed by HMC Architects, the award-winning, 78,657-SF facility accommodates 550 K-6 students and occupies a 9.68-acre site in the town center. The school's multi-purpose/fine arts building supplements the adjacent public library, recreation center, middle school, and shopping center, which constitute Carmel Valley's urban fabric. Public access playing fields and a landscaped promenade provide much-needed open space amid a dense urban district. Inside the one-story administration wing are a library/media center, computer laboratory, music classroom and theater, and the two-story classroom wings, which house nine small learning communities plus art and science classrooms. The interiors are equally creative. Each "community" includes a collaborative learning space, small breakout rooms, art display areas and direct outdoor access. Each space is oriented toward the library's circular reading room as the campus focal point. The environmental design principles embodied at Solana Pacific have been so successful that, in another civic gesture, the school district wants to teach "eco-friendly" ideas to students. Energy consumption at the school is 27-percent less than allowed by code.

Above: Courtyard.
Right: Auditorium.
Opposite top left: Classroom.
Opposite top right: Aerial view.
Opposite: Library.
Photography: Hewitt Garrison, and Durant Architectural Photography

HMC Architects

California State University, Fullerton
Kinesiology and Health Science Building
Fullerton, California

Opposite top: Lecture hall.
Left: Practice gymnasium.
Above: Exterior.
Right: Exterior detail.
Photography: Ryan Beck.

Upgrading and improving its campus to more adequately serve more than 30,000 career-, health-, and wellness-oriented students is the order of the day at California State University, Fullerton's 236-acre Orange County campus. As part of this agenda, the University's Kinesiology Department along with HMC Architects recently designed and constructed a 71,000-SF kinesiology and wellness center addition to its existing gymnasium building. In this new facility, students will prepare for future work in advanced health promotion, disease prevention, environmental and occupational health, safety, education, sports, therapeutic intervention, and fitness/wellness. The award-winning facility focuses on physical health through exercise and the study of human movement. It includes a two-story faculty office building, faculty support areas, and a department center. It also boasts a large mezzanine athletic area that overlooks the existing gymnasium with several adjacent multipurpose aerobic rooms. Under the mezzanine/aerobic areas are two floors that include a wellness center, a center for successful aging, several labs that focus on the study of human movement, and a 125-seat auditorium. Careful planning and staging of construction allowed the existing gymnasium to remain open while old faculty trailers were demolished and the new addition was built. The addition created a new quad for the campus that is anchored by the new Kinesiology Department. Near the entry court, aerobic and wellness activities are visible through strategically located windows, encouraging active, more healthful lifestyles. Students and staff feel invigorated when interacting and passing by this new area of campus.

HMC Architects

University of California, Riverside
Alumni & Visitors Center
Riverside, California

Situated near historic downtown Riverside, the University of California, Riverside (UCR) strongly values its history, neighbors, current student body, and alumnus. In keeping with this tone, UCR recently completed a new two-story, 12,300-SF alumni and visitors center. Bordered on one side by a secluded natural arroyo preserve and by a major campus entry road on the other, this new aesthetic now serves as a prominent public gateway to the campus, as well as a private facility to host alumni functions. Designed by HMC Architects, the building strives to recognize and celebrate this duality. As a vital component to the campus, the center serves as a bridge between life as a student and as an alumnus. It presents a formal face to the street with framed views to the campus, while shielding a more intimate setting for dining and event functions that take place on the arroyo side of the facility. The design is organized into predominantly public and private areas, which are oriented to corresponding public and private zones of the site. The building solution is a split-level scheme that minimizes the required cut and fill of the site, with the entry lobby and pre-function space located midway between the upper and lower floors. Meanwhile, a preserved sycamore tree becomes the anchor for an intimately scaled courtyard formed by the two wings of the building that embrace the arroyo. Adjacent to the dining areas, the commercial kitchen's location allows discreet delivery and service access while also being ideally located for any future expansion to the west. Weekend weddings and other events can be held at the center to offset operating expenses.

KlingStubbins

Philadelphia, PA
2301 Chestnut Street
Philadelphia, PA 19103
215.569.2900
215.569.5963 (Fax)

Washington, DC
2000 L Street, NW, Suite 215
Washington, DC 20036
202.785.5800
202.785.4755 (Fax)

Las Vegas, NV
3110 S. Rainbow Boulevard, Suite 104
Las Vegas, NV 89146
702.227.5983
702.227.5986 (Fax)

Cambridge, MA
1030 Massachusetts Avenue
Cambridge, MA 02138
617.491.6450
617.491.7104 (Fax)

Raleigh, NC
333 Fayetteville Street, Suite 1150
Raleigh, NC 27601
919.334.3111
919.334.3122 (Fax)

San Francisco, CA
153 Townsend Street, Suite 620
San Francisco, CA 94107
415.247.9701
415.247.9708 (Fax)

www.klingstubbins.com

KlingStubbins

University of Colorado at Denver and Health Sciences Center Research Complex I
Aurora, Colorado

Architecture seldom outshines the Rocky Mountains in Colorado, but the new, 622,000-square-foot Research Complex I at the University of Colorado at Denver and Health Sciences Center, on the Fitzsimons campus in Aurora, comes close. Of course, the two-part facility, comprising a nine-story North Building and 12-story South Building, has been designed by Kling, in association with Fentress Bradburn Architects, to address operational issues, including complex departmental relationships, the interface between research and clinical capacities, inexact boundaries between wet and dry spaces, and the implications of change over time. Consequently, space is organized into layered zones, based on 241 open and generic laboratory modules, which are supported by specialty laboratories, classrooms, conference rooms, and administrative offices. Core laboratories are generally centralized and developed around sophisticated equipment and specialized skills for the entire research community. Yet the environment is undeniably user-friendly. Education areas on the North Building's first floor bring students and researchers/faculty together. A 200-seat research auditorium and 100-seat education auditorium give audiences modern equipment and comfort. First- and second-level walkways join both buildings and lead to existing and future buildings. Daylight is maximized, along with spectacular views. John R. Sladek, University vice chancellor for research, concludes, "The facility is truly outstanding."

Top left: Two-level corridor.
Left: Evening view of exterior.
Top right: Laboratory.
Above: Auditorium.
Opposite: Exterior.
Photography: © Ron Johnson Photography.

KlingStubbins

North Carolina State University
David Clark Laboratories
Raleigh, North Carolina

Top left: Lounge.
Top right: Exterior.
Middle left: Laboratory.

Above left: Classroom.
Opposite: Atrium.
Photography: Jim West.

Design makes a difference in academia. This point is made daily at the David Clark Laboratories of North Carolina State University, in Raleigh, following a renovation and a 53,500-square foot addition, designed by The Stubbins Associates in association with Pearce, Brinkley, Cease & Lee. The University's Zoology Department had outgrown its existing facilities, which caused personnel, equipment and activities to be scattered across campus. For its new space the Zoology Department set goals that included consolidating the department in one location and providing teaching space, research space and offices to facilitate collaboration. The design comprises research and teaching laboratories, classrooms, offices, and laboratory support. It is organized so that spaces needing volume, such as laboratories, are installed in the new addition. Offices occupy space in the existing building with a two-story atrium linking the new and old sections of the building. A campus pathway runs through the site. Because of this configuration, students and faculty gather in the sunny atrium lobby before proceeding to their destinations, making the new addition feel welcoming and unified. In fact, the brick, precast concrete, aluminum and glass building looks so inviting students outside the program like studying in it too.

141

KlingStubbins

Case Western Reserve University
Cleveland Center for Structural Biology and Power
Partnership for Ohio Facility
Cleveland, Ohio

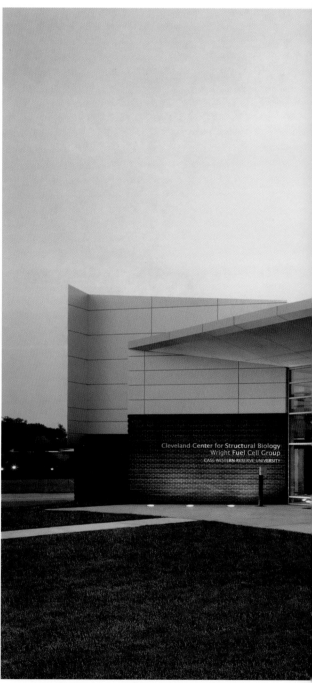

Lack of space on the 155-acre University Circle campus of Cleveland's Case Western Reserve University has led to the unusual pairing of two completely different research programs in one building, the new, one-story, 22,000-square-foot Cleveland Center for Structural Biology and Power Partnership for Ohio Facility, designed by KlingStubbins. The modern brick, glass and aluminum structure, which includes the Cleveland Center's nuclear magnetic resonance (NMR) facility, the Power Partnership's fuel cell laboratories, plus classrooms, offices, and conference/training room, succeeds through a plan that bisects the space with a boundary-defining circulation spine flowing directly from a shared lobby. Bringing together the two research groups yielded substantial time and cost savings for Case Western, an institution founded in 1826 that serves nearly 10,000 students. The pairing has also profoundly influenced the architecture. Space organization, utility design, and material selection, for example, reflect the careful placement of the NMR facility's 900 MHz magnet and five other magnets, which jointly create large, three-dimensional magnetic fields within the building and site. In addition, the massing and form showcase the duality inside, contrasting a series of radiating planes that reflect the forces within the NMR suite with a simple rectangular mass for the fuel cell laboratory.

Top left: Laboratory.
Top right: NMR Suite.
Opposite: Entrance.
Opposite left: Entry lobby.
Opposite right: Exterior.
Photography: © Shooting Star.

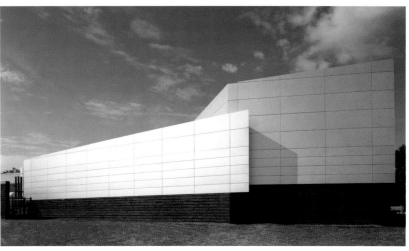

143

KlingStubbins

Harvard University Graduate School of Education
Cambridge, Massachusetts

In the process of master planning a major technology upgrade of Harvard University's Graduate School of Education it was determined that a simple and consistent user interface was key to successfully integrating advanced presentation and communications technologies into the daily life and pedagogy of the institution. Consequently, in designing for the wide variety of classroom, seminar and lecture spaces, The Stubbins Associates applied a limited pallet of screens, projectors, lighting and a common touch screen control panel. To ensure fail-safe operations, direct telephone connection to a help desk was provided in each room. Complementing the technology upgrades to the teaching spaces was the creation of a Media Center housing computer clusters, servers, operations personnel and spaces for experimentation. In all, the renovated facilities - classrooms, breakout spaces, offices, library, archives, conference rooms, lecture halls, computer laboratory, distance-learning classrooms and auditorium give the School tools to explore the myriad ways that technology will shape the future of teaching and learning.

Top left: Classroom.
Above: Computer lab.
Left: Conference room.
Bottom left: Lecture hall.
Photography: Warren Jagger.

144

Morphosis

2041 Colorado Avenue
Santa Monica, CA 90404
310.453.2247
310.829.3270 (Fax)
www.morphosis.net

Morphosis

Morphosis

University of Cincinnati Campus Recreation Center
Cincinnati, Ohio

Right: Sports hall.
Bottom right: Entry hall.
Opposite: MainStreet elevation.
Photography: Roland Halbe Architeckturfotografie.

If you're strolling along MainStreet, the contemporary district serving student academic and social interests at the University of Cincinnati, tracing a meandering path across the 137-acre West Campus from University Pavilion near the western edge to Jefferson Residence Complex on the east, you're unlikely to forget the moment when the new Campus Recreation Center comes into view. It's true that the car-free path, which evokes an Italian hill town, is densely populated by the work of distinguished architects. Even so, your attention is commanded by MainStreet's largest and most complex project, a 350,000-square-foot, multiuse facility, designed by 2005 Pritzker Prize laureate Thom Mayne of Morphosis with KZF Design as executive architect to house recreational facilities, classrooms, campus store, dining hall, aquatic center and student housing. The Center's three major components—Campus Recreation Center, MainStreet Lecture Rooms, and CRC Student Residence Hall—respond with originality and boldness to found conditions at the site.

146

Morphosis

Not only do they smoothe the transition between the sunken football field at Nippert Stadium and the higher grade of north campus, they also intensify the richness and dynamics of the surrounding space as they funnel students from the open expanse of the Campus Green through a narrow "pinch point" into the urban fabric of MainStreet. Equally important are the Center's interior spaces, representing a range of airy and effective facilities, outfitted with state-of-the-art equipment and accentuated by exposed structural elements, daylight from some three dozen skylights, and dramatic views of spaces above, below and outdoors. Among the highlights of the CRC complex are the six-court gymnasium with suspended, four-lane, 1/8-mile running track, 50-meter lap pool, leisure pool, whirlpool, two one-meter and one three-meter diving boards, cardio-fitness facilities, 40-foot climbing wall, three multi-purpose rooms, eight racquet courts, lockers, pro shop, six electronic classrooms, 400-seat CenterCourt point-of-service restaurant, 180-seat Stadium View Café

Top left: Weightlifting room.

Right: Evening view of recreational and housing components.

Morphosis

overlooking Nippert Stadium, 4,000-square-foot Market on Main convenience store, and 224-bed, suite-style CRC Student Residence Hall, which stands on pilotis above the rest of the complex. While much has already been accomplished on campus to transform the University of Cincinnati from a commuter school, founded in 1819 with

Top: Competition pool.
Far left: Classroom.
Left: Corridor.
Opposite: Restaurant.

Morphosis

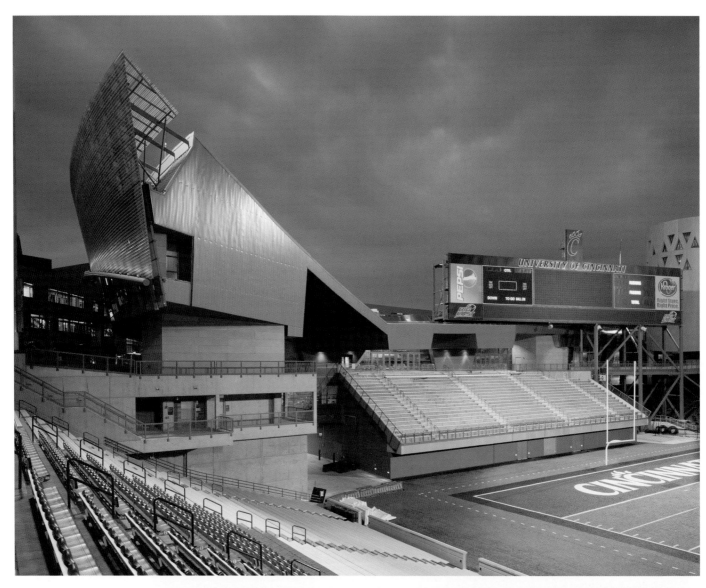

the chartering of Cincinnati College and the Medical College of Ohio, into what the Carnegie Commission ranks as one of America's top 25 public research universities, the completion of MainStreet—through the addition of the Campus Recreation Center—could be easily regarded as saving the best for last.

Top: Stadium.
Right: Pool and housing component.

Payette

285 Summer Street
Boston, MA 02210
617.895.1000
617.895.1002 (Fax)
www.payette.com

Payette

Oberlin College
Science Center
Oberlin, Ohio

Musicians rightly consider Oberlin College's Conservatory of Music, founded in 1865, one of the world's finest music schools. What they may not know is that 173-year-old Oberlin, based in Oberlin, Ohio, 35 miles southwest of Cleveland, also produces more undergraduates who ultimately receive doctorates in the sciences than any other undergraduate college. To enhance its science education, the College recently remodeled Kettering Hall, Sperry Neuroscience Wing, and Wright Laboratory of Physics, and augmented them with new construction, resulting in the three-level, 230,209-square-foot Science Center. With an award-winning design by Payette, the complex offers such state-of-the-art facilities for the biology, chemistry, neuroscience and physics departments as 25- to 40-seat classrooms that act like laboratories, 230-seat, surround-sound-equipped West Lecture Hall, a multi-media-rich science library, versatile laboratories and computer laboratories, and a sunlit, two-story Commons and café to bring students and faculty members together. But you needn't be a science student to enjoy one of the Center's major benefits. By removing the east half of Kettering Hall to accommodate the new scheme, the Center has breached a "great wall of science" that acted as a north-south barrier on campus, inviting the entire Oberlin community to stroll through its "village of buildings."

Top right: Exterior at twilight.
Top left: Library.
Below left: Lecture hall.
Bottom left: The Commons.
Opposite: Seminar room.
Photography: Jeff Goldberg/ Esto Photographics.

Payette

Ohio Wesleyan University
Conrades Wetherell Science Center
Delaware, Ohio

While science students and faculty at Ohio Wesleyan University are the major beneficiaries of the new Conrades Wetherell Science Center, located on the 164-year-old, Methodist-affiliated school's 200-acre campus in Delaware, Ohio, they're not the only ones. The mission of the three-story, 155,267-square-foot complex, created by refurbishing two 1960s buildings and expanding them by 54,317 square feet, has been to unite the laboratory sciences, facilitating additional growth, expanding space for research, and instilling a sense of place among the science community. Yet the Center, comprising laboratories, lecture halls, classrooms, offices, lounges, science library and atrium, also creates an attractive destination at the east end of a long east-west axis that was considered remote. Its design deliberately blurs the edges of resident depart-

ments, including botany, chemistry, computer science, geography, geology, mathematics, physics and zoology, so no one department occupies an entire floor or wing, and students and faculty members are encouraged to meet in corridors, stairs and conveniently placed lounges. The Center's attractive new atrium and café, turning the space between new and existing wings into a gathering place, does even more. Attracting students from all disciplines, they have placed the sciences firmly in the mainstream of campus life.

Top left: Exterior of two original buildings.

Left: Exterior of addition at night.

Top right: Faculty office.

Above: Laboratory.

Opposite: Atrium.

Photography: Warren Jagger.

Payette

West Virginia University
Life Sciences Building
Morgantown, West Virginia

Towering like a rocky outcrop above a steep slope of West Virginia University's 913-acre Morgantown campus overlooking the Monongahela River, the new Life Sciences Building powerfully defines a new quadrangle for the school's Lower Bowl, some three stories below the main campus elevation. The bold, elongated form and formidable mass of the seven-story, 196,000-square-foot brick, glass and copper-clad structure, designed by Payette consolidates the biology and psychology departments, the two largest programs in the Eberly College of Arts and Sciences. It also provides general purpose classrooms for the 139-year-old University, and negotiates a transition between a formal, ceremonial quadrangle to the south and a low-scale residential area to the north. Inside, a spacious, open and naturally lighted environment accommodates classrooms, laboratories, 125- and 250-seat auditoriums, a community mental health center, animal quarters, an herbarium, a greenhouse, and a continuous glazed gallery running the length of the building at the main teaching floor. The general purpose facilities occupy the ground floor and life sciences facilities and are positioned above and below. In complimenting the design, Nellis Duane, dean of Eberly College, reports, "The building, with all of the windows and light, creates a very positive environment for learning and research."

Top: South elevation.
Above left: Corridor.
Above: Lecture hall.
Left: Laboratory.
Opposite: South elevation south west corner.
Photography: Warren Jagger.

Payette

University of Maryland School of Medicine
Health Sciences Facility, Phase II
Baltimore, Maryland

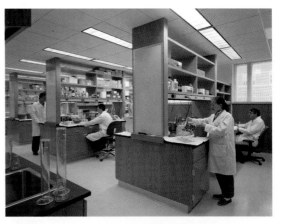

Can you name the venerable Baltimore institution that represents America's first public and fifth oldest medical school, as well as the first to institute a residency-training program? It's the University of Maryland School of Medicine, established in 1807 as the founding school of the University. The School of Medicine thrives today as an integral component of the University of Maryland, Baltimore's 60-acre campus. The completion of the new, six-story, 192,000-square-foot Health Sciences Facility, Phase II, designed by Payette with Design Collective, Inc., illustrates how the School continues to reshape the University as it grows. Delivering new research space and equipment to advance various health sciences programs for the State of Maryland and the University, the stately, brick-clad building features a curving limestone-clad wall designed to frame a new campus green in downtown Baltimore. The scheme is used to advantage inside as well as outside. Faculty offices are grouped on each floor along the curved wall, flanking shared conference rooms. They form a distinct zone within interiors characterized by neighborhoods conducive to informal and serendipitous interaction, and modular laboratories that expand from four- to eight-person facilities when flexibility is required. As for the outside, what city wouldn't welcome more greenery?

Left: Exterior.
Top right: Laboratory.
Above: Main entry.

Photography: Alan Karchmer, Robert Creamer.

Perkins Eastman

115 Fifth Avenue
New York, NY 10003
212.353.7200
212.353.7676 (Fax)
www.perkinseastman.com

Arlington, VA
Charlotte, NC
Chicago, IL
Dubai, UAE
Oakland, CA
Pittsburgh, PA
Shanghai, PRC
Stamford, CT
Toronto, ON

Perkins Eastman

Perkins Eastman

University of Connecticut
Stamford Campus
Stamford, Connecticut

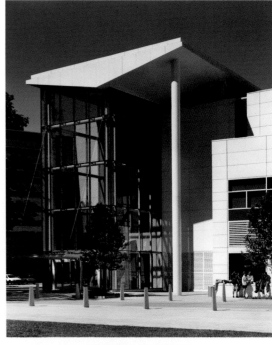

A marketplace of ideas has supplanted a marketplace of fashion at the University of Connecticut's radiant new Stamford Campus, designed by Perkins Eastman. This inspired exercise in adaptive reuse transforms the reinforced concrete structure that once supported a branch of Bloomingdale's, the high-end fashion retailer, into a versatile, three-story, 254,000-square-foot learning environment. Incorporated are a library, classrooms, conference rooms, auditoriums, computer learning centers, bookstore, art gallery, and offices. As the new centerpiece of UConn's Stamford campus, it enables the school to build strong ties to the community and corporations in the area, which boasts one of the nation's highest concentrations of corporate headquarters, including those of such Fortune 500 companies as Xerox, Pitney Bowes, Crane, Rayonier, General Reinsurance, and Tosco. The conversion from department store to academic center had its complications, to be sure. The deep floors that housed Bloomingdale's have been dramatically opened up by a three-story glass addition enclosing a public concourse or "main street" along the public thoroughfare that invigorates the neighborhood day and night, and two atrium spaces or "light spines" that cut diagonally through all three floors to brighten circulation and major program areas. Happily, the interior design, featuring modern furnishings and finishes in a neutral color palette accented by red chairs, naturally finished wood desktops and cabinetry, and colorful banners displaying UConn's school colors, is a match for the architecture. Students in the southern Connecticut city of some 117,000 residents and the surrounding region are quickly taking advantage of UConn's new opportunities, so the current enrollment of some 1,600 students, ranging in age from late teens to adult with more than half holding day jobs, is projected to reach 2,800. Perhaps it's the executive MBA program, requiring just 18 months of weekend study, that attracts them. Then again, it might be the building.

Top left: Exterior.
Top right: Exterior detail.
Above: Staircase.
Opposite: Main Public Concourse.
Photography: Chuck Choi.

162

Perkins Eastman

St. John's University
DaSilva Academic Center
Staten Island, New York

College students forego campus life by heading home right after class. That's why the Staten Island, New York campus of St. John's University, a leading Catholic university founded in 1870, has high hopes for the new, three-story, 40,000-square-foot John DaSilva Academic Center, designed by Perkins Eastman. Occupying the site of a former parking lot along with a new campus green, DaSilva Academic Center helps unite a student body of commuters and campus residents by establishing a destination for the entire student body. Its strategically located site, for example, is visible from all campus entry points. Trading monumental-ity for accessibility, its striking façade breaks open the building's solid mass with expansive glass curtainwalls to draw attention to its activities. Inside, its two-story, glass-enclosed entry lobby represents a tempting gathering place, while the first floor's technology center, featuring computer laboratories arranged along a single-loaded, glazed corridor, draws students late into the night and on weekends. The second floor offers classrooms, science and communications labora-tories, administrative suite and a student study lounge, and the third floor houses individual faculty offices and a faculty lounge overlook-ing the lounge below. One building alone can't sustain campus life, but DaSilva Academic Center definitely alters the scene.

Above left: Lobby.
Left: Western elevation.
Below: Exterior at dusk.
Photography: Chuck Choi.

164

Perkins Eastman

University at Albany, State University of New York
The Boor Sculpture Building
Albany, New York

Above: Doorway.
Right: Exterior at dusk.
Below right: Workshop.
Bottom: Auditorium entrance.
Photography: Chuck Choi.

A custom electric monorail transporting up to 5,000 pounds of materials from an exterior work pad to interior metal and kiln areas, passing through a 14-foot-high Dutch door, may not immediately conjure images of art masterpieces in the making, but it's a key component in the The Boor Sculpture Building at the State University of New York at Albany. The one-story, 20,000-square-foot structure, designed by Perkins Eastman, fulfills its mission with such efficiency and artistry that the brick, glass and zinc-paneled walls and cantilevered rain canopy, which shelter state-of-the-art metalworking, foundry, kiln, woodshop and multimedia facilities, collectively resemble a work of sculpture. Its award-winning appearance stems from creating appropriate spaces for artists and their materials that are exciting in their own right. Thus, a central block housing all workshops, each arranged to follow the natural sequence inherent in its work processes, forms the heart of the space, highlighted by a zinc-paneled main black box gallery/lecture space and flanked on two sides by graduate studios. Though sculpture is just one of many subjects pursued by the 17,000 students at SUNY Albany's 10 schools and colleges on three campuses, this impressive new facility proclaims the respect sculpture deserves and receives.

Perkins Eastman

Roger Ludlowe Middle School
Fairfield, Connecticut

Above: Library exterior at dusk.
Far left: Auditorium.
Left: Auditorium lobby.
Opposite: Classroom exterior at dusk.
Photography: Woodruff/Brown.

What does a superior public school system require? Fairfield, Connecticut provides excellent professional staff, good support systems and modern, well-equipped facilities. Yet the affluent community of over 57,300 residents, hailed by *Money* Magazine as the Northeast's "best place to live" in 2006, marshals its resources prudently. Roger Ludlowe

Middle School, established in a renovated building in 1998 as the third of three middle schools, only recently acquired a new, three-story, 200,000-square-foot facility of its own, designed by Perkins Eastman. Although its former home is on its way to becoming Fairfield Ludlowe High School, as one of two existing facilities Perkins Eastman is renovating for the

school district (along with Fairfield Warde High School), it remains a close neighbor on a two-school campus, sharing many athletic facilities. The award-winning new facility gives 775 students, grades 6-8, a spacious, naturally illuminated and effective learning environment, nonetheless. The attractive, L-shaped, double-loaded structure, containing a

1,000-seat gymnasium and auxiliary half-court gymnasium, library/media center, 650-seat auditorium, cafeteria, administrative offices and support spaces as well as classrooms, occupies a slope on the site, reducing its apparent size and minimizing its visibility from an adjoining residential street. From its finely detailed exterior of brick, glass and

Perkins Eastman

wood to its lively interior of contemporary furnishings, stimulating colors and natural wood finishes, the school also celebrates modern life and traditional residential architecture in Fairfield.

Top: Classroom exterior.
Above: Library.
Right: Exterior detail.
Photography: Woodruff/Brown.

Perkins+Will

800.837.9455
www.perkinswill.com
schools@perkinswill.com

Atlanta
Boston
Charlotte
Chicago
Dallas
Hartford
Houston
Los Angeles
Miami
Minneapolis
New York
Research Triangle Park
San Francisco
Seattle
Vancouver
Victoria
Washington D.C.

Perkins+Will

Perspectives Charter School
Chicago, Illinois

Jacketed in corrugated metal and glass, Perspectives Charter School is a new, two-story, 30,000-square-foot school for 350 students, grades 6-12, that's tough enough for Chicago's industrial South Loop neighborhood. But the award-winning building, designed by Perkins+Will, has a compassionate heart. Founded in 1997 by Chicago teachers Kim Day and Diana Shulla-Cose, Perspectives provides urban students with a rigorous and relevant education, achieving results so outstanding—100 percent of the Class of 2004 graduated and 95 percent went to college—that 500 students are currently on the waiting list for admission. The school, encompassing a library, lunch room/assembly space or family room, science laboratories, computer laboratory, teachers lounge and office space as well as classrooms for middle school on the first

floor and high school on the second, represents the physical embodiment of its curriculum, "A Disciplined Life." Its distinctive form, shaped by a tight, triangular site, gives a diverse community of students a sense of identity and security, a structured and supportive environment, and economical yet inspiring facilities revolving around the two-story family room as physical and spiritual center. Declares Rodney Justin, president of Perspectives' board of directors, "Our students finally have a place they are proud to call home."

Top: Media center.

Left: Exterior of media center.

Above: Main entry.

Bottom left: Aerial view of site.

Opposite: Family room in balcony view.

Photography: James Steinkamp.

171

Perkins+Will

Alpharetta High School
Alpharetta, Georgia

Scale and security preoccupy so many school planners that Perkins+Will suggested the new Alpharetta High School, in Alpharetta, Georgia, serve as a "school within a school" by housing 2,100 students in three 700-student academic houses. With Fulton County public school officials in accord, Perkins+Will has designed the 330,000-square-foot school so each "house" of students grades 9-12 and core teachers taps into a linear spine connecting such shared functions as the cafeteria, media center, theater, athletic facilities, IT, family and consumer sciences, electronic media production and professional food services. The three-part facility, comprising a three-level main building, two-level arts/administration wing and two-level gymnasium, all clad in brick, glass and metal shingle, occupies the high point of a steeply sloping site, along with terraced parking areas and playing fields, to minimize site disturbance. Alpharetta High recognizes local conditions in numerous other ways, placing athletics and arts facilities at the front door to facilitate public access, juxtaposing the cafeteria and media center so library overflow can spill into the cafeteria, and embracing environmental design through construction techniques, building materials, storm water management and energy consumption. *The Atlanta Journal Constitution* rightly praised the school as "a lesson in good architecture."

Top left: Front perspective.
Top right: Corridor.
Above: Cafeteria exterior.
Opposite: Cafeteria.
Photography: Chris A. Little (interiors), Chris Barrett/Hedrich Blessing (exteriors).

Perkins+Will

Blythewood High School
Blythewood, South Carolina

Can a school large enough to accommodate 1,700 students feel small enough to give students the individual attention they need? Faced with the rapid growth of its school age population, Richland School District in suburban Columbia, South Carolina, a progressive, nationally-recognized school district, wanted a new high school that would support quality education through small learning communities, provide student gathering places and a collegiate atmosphere, promote parent involvement, facilitate community use, and integrate technology. The participatory programming process that laid the foundation for Blythewood High School, involving administrators, teachers, staff, students, school board members and community representatives along with architects and planners, paid off handsomely with the fall 2005 opening of the award-winning, two-story, 294,076-square-foot facility, designed by Perkins+Will in association with The Boudreaux Group. It is a formidable school by any measure, including classrooms, music/art/drama classrooms, career-technology laboratories, media center, cafeteria, cybercafé, 2,000-seat collegiate basketball gymnasium, auxiliary gymnasium, 6,000-seat district-wide football stadium and playing fields for baseball, football, softball, tennis and track and field. But its size and comprehensiveness are used unconventionally to create a series of smaller schools, giving Blythewood four thematic "houses" of classrooms or small learning communities (SLCs). Based on their individual interests, students in each house select from a variety of career clusters and majors including: business management, government and public service, health science and human services, and information technology to name a few. Each SLC is accompanied by satellite administrative and faculty planning areas supporting various professional learning communities (PLCs). While also sharing the use of two other major resources: a science and

Top Left: Main entry.

Above: Lakeside view of exterior.

Opposite bottom left: Cyber café.

Opposite bottom right: Culinary careers adjacent to cybercafé.

Photography: James Steinkamp.

174

Perkins+Will

Blythewood High School
Blythewood, South Carolina

career technology laboratories wing, coupling conventional science laboratories to large, high-bay, utility-rich career technology laboratories to sustain their natural synergies, and a nucleus of central community spaces that include central administration, health clinic and student activities center, surrounding the main lobby at the heart of the school to give students, faculty, staff and the community easy access. The four houses also share a breathtaking amenity few schools can boast: a natural pond that is part of the 138-acre wetlands site's drainage system. Blythewood principal Dr. Sharon Buddin proudly observes, "This school is designed to be a true Breaking Ranks II high school."

Top left: Lobby.
Above: Carrer technology lab.
Right: Locker bay.
Photography: James Steinkamp.

176

Research Facilities Design

3965 Fifth Avenue
Suite 300
San Diego, CA 92103-3107
619.297.0159
619.294.4901 (Fax)
www.rfd.com

Research Facilities Design

Agnes Scott College
Mary Brown Bullock Science Center
Decatur, Georgia

To be handed the keys to a new, state-of-the-art science building that is flexible and multi-functional is an aspiration shared by many schools. Fortunately for Agnes Scott College, in Decatur, Georgia, its wish was recently fulfilled through a new facility designed by Shepley Bulfinch Richardson Abbott, architect, and Research Facilities Design, laboratory building design consultant. Mary Brown Bullock Science Center gives the indepen-

dent, liberal arts college for women, founded in 1889, a three-story, 117,986-square-foot, brick-clad building with teaching and research laboratories, laboratory support, animal facility, greenhouse, electronic microscopy suite, classrooms and offices for biology, chemistry, physics and psychology. Modular teaching, research and support spaces, organized in clusters by department, and offices grouped adjacent to the building's three-story

central atrium let occupants respond to the changing needs of their disciplines while encouraging inter-disciplinary collaboration, recruitment and retention among faculty and students. There's scientific drama as well: The atrium's focal point is a mural depicting the DNA sequence from a living direct female descendent of the school's founder, Agnes Scott. Assessing the design team's contribution, Sandra Bowden, professor of biology and

"project shepherd," states, "You helped us to design and build a truly wonderful place for teaching and research."

Below: Physics teaching.
Bottom left: Lab with tables.
Bottom right: Exterior.
Opposite top left: Corridor.
Opposite top right: Chemistry teaching lab with glass fume hoods.
Opposite bottom: Faculty/student research laboratory.
Photography: Robert Canfield.

Research Facilities Design

University of Missouri-Columbia
Christopher S. Bond Life Sciences Center
Columbia, Missouri

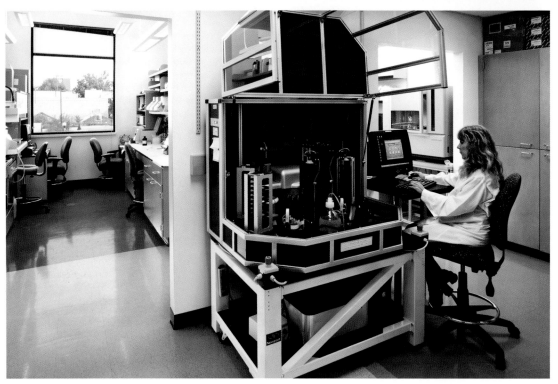

LAMMABLE
Keep Fire
Away

One size rarely fits all whatever we measure, but the University of Missouri's new Christopher S. Bond Life Sciences Center comes close. The five-story, 207,000-square-foot facility, designed by Anshen + Allen Architects, design architect, BNIM Architects, executive architect, and Research Facilities Design, laboratory building design consultant, features interdisciplinary research facilities shared by the College of Agriculture, Food and Natural Resources, College of Arts and Sciences, College of Veterinary Medicine, College of Human and Environmental Sciences, and School of Medicine. Its dexterity stems from a series of three-module open research laboratories with island benches, technician desks along exterior window walls, and fume hood/equipment alcoves along corridor walls. While laboratories can be separated by partial partitions for limited privacy, door/wall assemblies can be installed for full privacy, and laboratory support spaces across corridors can accommodate specialized functions. Large and complex as the Center is, with 50 generic modular life science research laboratories, three biosciences teaching laboratories, core facilities, animal facility, insectary, growth suite, greenhouses, auditorium, conference rooms, cyber café, and faculty offices, all housed in two laboratory wings separated by an atrium and office wing, it draws constant praise from occupants and visitors alike.

Top left: Cyber Café.
Top right: Research Laboratory.
Above left: Exterior.
Above: Core DNA facility.
Opposite bottom left: Atrium.
Opposite bottom right: Interaction space.
Photography: Robert Canfield.

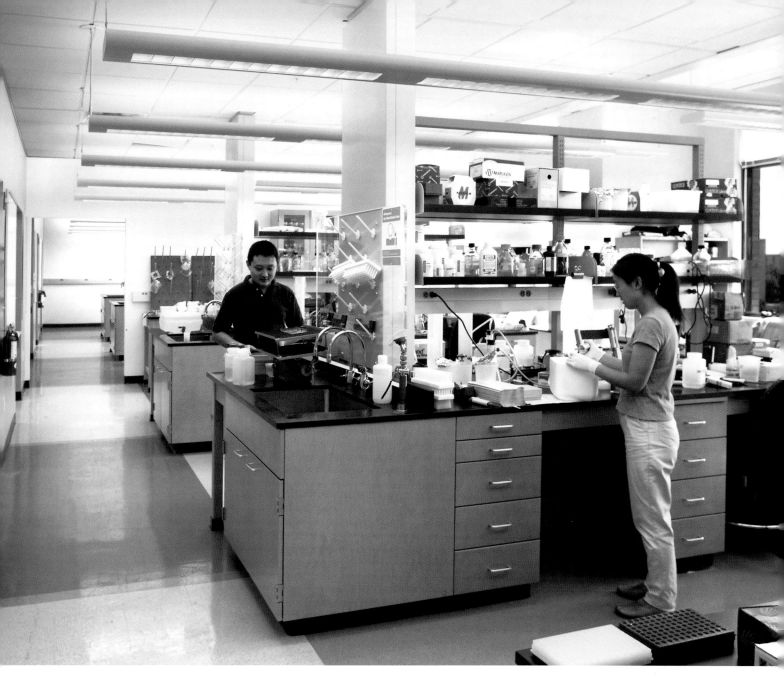

Research Facilities Design

University of Kentucky
Ralph G. Anderson Building
Lexington, Kentucky

Right: Mechanical Engineering Teaching Lab.

Far right: Mechanical Engineer-research lab with optic tables.

Below right: Exterior.

Opposite top: Water Flume Laboratory.

Opposite bottom: Anechoic test chamber.

Photography: Robert Canfield.

Shiny Toyotas rolling out of a Georgetown, Kentucky plant help explain why the University of Kentucky's new Ralph G. Anderson Building could not be better timed. The four-story, 114,800-square-foot mechanical engineering facility, designed by Anshen + Allen Architects, design architect, Taylor Whitney Architects, executive architect, and Research Facilities Design, laboratory building design consultant, houses laboratories for graduate research and undergraduate education, including automo-tive laboratories able to accept multiple running motors as well as full-size cars, along with such spaces as an anechoic chamber, subsonic wind tunnel, classrooms, student career/resource center, conference rooms, and offices of the Department of Mechanical Engineering. The project is the latest step in the University's plan to provide world-class facilities for its College of Engineering. Yet the design transcends function to establish a stimulating educational environment. Not only does the brick and limestone-clad structure recreate a venerable engineering quadrangle, its amenities include a glass-enclosed atrium between its two blocks, an adjoining outdoor courtyard, and a student commons area for study and social interaction. For the 26,000 students on UK's 687-acre campus adjacent to downtown Lexington, it's a reminder of engineering's continuing importance in an institution founded as Agricultural and Mechanical College in 1865.

Research Facilities Design

University of San Diego
Donald P. Shiley Center for Science & Technology
San Diego, California

Spanish Renaissance-inspired architecture imparts a distinctive, Old World charm to the splendidly landscaped, 180-acre campus of the University of San Diego, a Catholic institution chartered in 1949 that currently serves over 7,500 students. But looks can be deceiving. The University's academic activities are thoroughly up to date—as can be discerned in the new, four-story, 150,000-square-foot Donald P. Shiley Center for Science & Technology, designed by Carrier Johnson with Research Facilities Design as laboratory building design consultant. Within its Spanish Renaissance-style exterior are advanced teaching and research laboratories, laboratory support, classrooms, and offices for the departments of biology, chemistry, physics, and marine and environmental studies, plus a rooftop greenhouse and aquaculture facility, small animal facility, NMR laboratory and hazardous materials specimen storage facility. Fortunately, the Center does more than provide modern accommodations by promoting a collaborative teaching and learning environment, encouraging interaction between faculty and students, and maintaining long-term operational flexibility. Examples of its sensitivity can be seen in the teaching and research laboratories, whose modular design, wood casework, flexible layouts and fume hoods accommodate a range of disciplines to support interdisciplinary teaching and research, and the atrium's hanging sculpture, featuring elements of physical, biological and marine sciences all working together.

Top left: Faculty/student project laboratory.

Top right: Life science teaching laboratory.

Above right: Science on display.

Right: Research aquarium.

Photography: Robert Canfield.

184

Sasaki Associates Inc.

64 Pleasant Street
Watertown, MA 02472
617.926.3300
617.924.2748 (Fax)
www.sasaki.com

77 Geary Street
4th Floor
San Francisco, CA 94108
415.776.7272
415.202.7403 (Fax)

Sasaki Associates Inc.

Sasaki Associates Inc.

Utah State University
Manon Caine Russell and Kathryn Caine Wanlass Performance Hall
Logan, Utah

Spectacular natural landscape surrounds some 23,000 students at Utah State University, located in the city of Logan in northern Utah's Cache Valley, where the 450-acre campus is flanked by mountains, lakes, rivers and ski resorts. Recently, the land-grant institution, founded in 1888, acquired an impressive landmark of its own: the 420-seat Manon Caine Russell and Kathryn Caine Wanlass Performance Hall, designed by Sasaki Associates. Not only does the 20,000-square-foot structure rise like a mountain range over its piazza, it reinforces Utah State's historic com-

mitment to arts education by providing a dramatic venue with superb acoustics for chamber music and the spoken word. A product of careful studies in sound quality and theater technology, the facility is anchored by an orthogonal concrete shell of 18-inch thick concrete walls that encloses the main performance space. This shell contrasts sharply with the glass and zinc-clad entrance pavilion, whose origami-like folded volumes evoke the nearby Bear River Mountains, and the hall's interior, whose walls are layered with drywall and finished in beech wood veneer. Man-made wonder

that it is, the design also delivers on its promise with acoustics so exceptional that University musician-in-residence Russell Fallstad, a violist, declared, "Our hall is a Stradivarius."

Top left: Auditorium.
Above: Exterior at twilight.
Right: Lobby.
Opposite botom right: Aerial view of exterior.
Photography: Robert Benson Photography.

Sasaki Associates Inc.

Harvard University
Hemenway Gymnasium
Cambridge, Massachusetts

Old as they may appear, many buildings on the Cambridge, Massachusetts campus of Harvard University, founded in 1636, may be replacements for even older predecessors. Still, age didn't prevent the recent renovation of Hemenway Gymnasium, designed by Sasaki Associates, from following an aggressive, fast-track schedule, despite the demands of clients and landmark preservationists. A recreational fitness facility originally designed by Coolidge, Shepley, Bulfinch and Abbott and completed in 1938, Hemenway occupies an historic district bordering Cambridge Green on one side and Harvard Law School on the other, adjacent to Harvard Yard. While not Harvard's main athletic facility, the three-level, 28,000-square-foot building is fondly remembered by generations of students. For the makeover, the interior was completely reorganized with minor alternations to the original structure, replacing seven American-size squash courts with three international-size ones, doubling the supply of fitness equipment, consolidating locker rooms, reinstalling a top level gymnasium, along with a multi-purpose room replacing a former badminton court, and introducing air conditioning. Unlike its former self, the new Hemenway is efficient, navigable and filled with daylight, using its main stairway to let patrons survey its entire space. One obvious concession to modernity is deliberately understated, however—a new elevator, meeting ADA standards.

Top left: Exterior at twilight.
Top right: Gymnasium.
Left: Stairway.
Photography: Robert Benson Photography.

Sasaki Associates Inc.

University of California, Davis
Segundo Commons
Davis, California

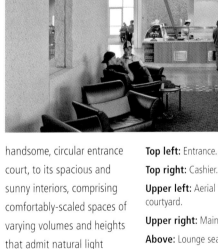

Students complain about campus food so persistently that response to the new Segundo Commons at University of California, Davis from many of its 29,637 students has left school officials pleasantly surprised. Everyone raves about the one-story, 49,000-square-foot, stone, precast concrete and glass-clad building, designed by Sasaki Associates, which serves the Segundo housing district on the 5,300-acre campus. Segundo Commons profoundly differs from its predecessor. Not only does it raise capacity to almost 900 diners, it provides cutting-edge food preparation technologies that make it the new central kitchen for all UC Davis dining commons. It is also a marketplace dining service that distributes finishing and serving stations throughout dining areas, and a choice of accommodations that includes soft seating in the lounge area as well as table seating in one of three carpeted dining sections, and even a deli-style self-service area for take-out food. Equally important, it provides an appealing environment for the enjoyment of food and conversation, from its curving exterior form, focused on a handsome, circular entrance court, to its spacious and sunny interiors, comprising comfortably-scaled spaces of varying volumes and heights that admit natural light from windows, curtain walls, skylights and clerestories. In fact, Segundo Commons looks good enough to eat.

Top left: Entrance.
Top right: Cashier.
Upper left: Aerial view of courtyard.
Upper right: Main dining room.
Above: Lounge seating area.
Photography: David Wakely, Timothy Rue (upper left).

Sasaki Associates Inc.

University of Pennsylvania
Penn Connects: A Vision for the Future
Philadelphia, Pennsylvania

University of Pennsylvania President Amy Gutmann's inaugural goal, set in 2004, was to "engage locally and globally." However, the Schuylkill River and subsequently the Northeast railroad corridor have separated this venerable Ivy League institution from Center City since its relocation in 1870. With little room to grow in dense West Philadelphia, the school of some 20,000 students now controls enough key parcels on the Schuylkill's east bank to develop a 45-acre East Campus. Retained to create a multi-decade master plan that will expand capabilities in medicine, research and the arts and forge a link to Center City, Sasaki Associates has proposed a visionary scheme featuring vast green open public spaces. Elaborating on the themes of engagement and connection, the plan conceives the East Campus as a coherent unit of four "bridges," actual and metaphorical. A "Living/Learning Bridge" establishes a strong Walnut Street axis joined to Rittenhouse Square and the rest of Center City. A "Sports/Recreation Bridge" envisions a new pedestrian-only cable-stay span accompanied by sports and recreation parks along the Schuylkill and similar amenities. A "Health Sciences/Cultural Bridge" at South Street and future "Research Bridge" will sustain new health care and research initiatives critical to Penn's—and Philadelphia's—future.

Top left: View from Center City towards the Penn campus.

Top right: View of recreation fields and the Schuylkill River Pedestrian Bridge.

Above: Vision for the east campus area.

Upper left: Proposed Hill Square College House.

Left: New fields, public spaces and development at the east campus area.

Bottom left: Bridges of connectivity.

Illustration: Courtesy of Sasaki Associates.

Sasaki Associates Inc.

University of California, Berkeley
Landscape Heritage Plan
Berkeley, California

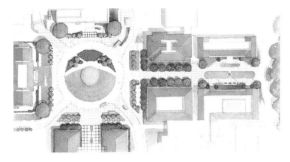

Proclaiming the enduring power of inspired design and enlightened philanthropy, the Beaux-Arts style Classical Core at the University of California, Berkeley campus remains one of America's largest and finest assemblages of Beaux-Arts buildings and landscape. Born of an international competition sponsored by Phoebe Apperson Hearst and won by Emile Bénard of Paris, the Classical Core is sited along an east/west axis that affords views towards the Golden Gate Bridge and the Pacific Ocean, joining California's oldest academic institution (founded in 1868) to the nation's westward expansion. Sasaki Associates' role in developing the school's Landscape Heritage Plan is to preserve the Core's historic legacy while enhancing the setting and accommodating growth. For example, among the many ideas for preserving and enhancing the Core, the Plan proposes measures for the Mining Circle/Oppenheimer Way, the eastern anchor of the East/West Central Glade and a defining idea of the campus envisioned by Frederick Law Olmsted, that includes restoring the central pool, incorporating a central path within the circle, unifying the space with consistent paving, and planting London plane trees to reinforce the plaza's square form. Thus, the Plan perpetuates landscape's role, providing a naturalistic counterpoint to buildings, into the University's second century.

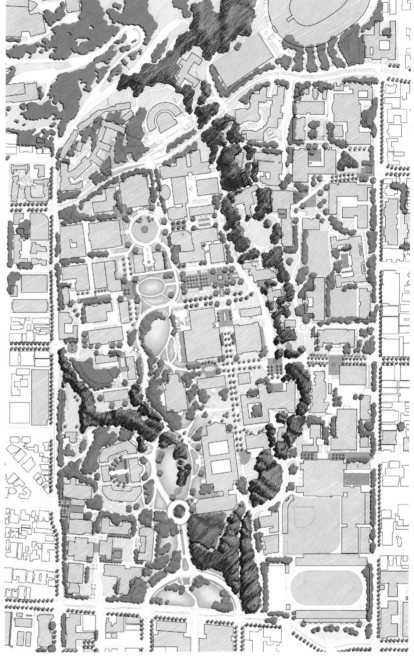

Top left: Mining Circle concept plan.

Top right: Master plan.

Above left: Mining Circle design.

Right: The Circle.

Illustration: Courtesy of Sasaki Associates.

191

Sasaki Associates Inc.

St. Edward's University
Landscape Master Plan
Austin, Texas

Can the cherished popular view of a university campus as a lushly landscaped and tree-shaded Elysium coexist with the unyielding regional climate surrounding a revered private liberal arts institution on a hilltop overlooking Austin, Texas? For St. Edward's University, a school founded in 1885 that serves some 4,900 students, the answer is an overwhelming yes. In keeping with goals established by St. Edward's, Sasaki Associates has produced a Landscape Master Plan to guide campus landscaping over the next two decades while instituting conservation measures that respond to the unique climatic conditions of Texas Hill Country. The Plan envisions a regionally appropriate landscape based on water conservation and microclimate enhancement, so that over 60 percent of the campus will be maintained as a non-irrigated dry climate landscape. Simultaneously, the scheme will introduce inviting, shaded outdoor spaces oriented to local solar and wind orientation as well as Austin's year-round outdoor lifestyle. To this end, courtyards, gateways and informal, tree-shaded gathering spots are among the new elements proposed. Trees at the campus's perimeter and along the streets will serve double duty, defining boundaries and mitigating the urban island heat. The scheme should comfort and sustain St. Edwards for years to come.

Top: View to main building from the new Oak Grove at Trustee Hall.
Middle left: Holy Cross Plaza.
Middle right: Holy Cross Plaza.
Bottom left: Courtyard at Dujarie Residential Hall.
Bottom right: Fountain plaza.
Photography: Craig Kuhner.

Skidmore, Owings & Merrill LLP

14 Wall Street
New York, NY 10005
212.298.9300
212.298.9500 (Fax)
www.SOM.com

Skidmore, Owings & Merrill LLP

Skidmore, Owings & Merrill LLP

Deerfield Academy
Koch Center for Science, Mathematics and Technology
Deerfield, Massachusetts

Just as the sycamore tree stands taller and fuller now before the Academy Building, where it was flourishing on March 1, 1797, the day Deerfield Academy officially opened, the 280-acre campus of the venerable preparatory school in Deerfield, Massachusetts has matured into a tightly-knit and picturesque academic village for 608 students. Pride of place is certainly evident in Deerfield's largest and most complex building project to date, the new, three-story, 80,000-square Koch Center for Science, Mathematics and Technology, designed by Skidmore, Owings & Merrill. The Koch Center achieves two basic goals: the creation of an interdisciplinary facility for mathematics and science, and the unification and connection of the campus. As a learning environment, the modern, brick-clad building comes well equipped, with a three-story atrium and two wings housing classrooms, laboratories, 225-seat auditorium, planetarium, lounges, café, and outdoor terrace. As a topographical feature, the award-winning structure gracefully straddles the grade changes between the upper and lower campus levels on its site, using the site's contour lines to trace the main walls of the building and blend with the landscape. Eric Widmer, Deerfield historian and former headmaster, has proudly noted, "This is the largest and most ambitious project the school has ever undertaken."

Top: View of exterior from playing feild.

Above left: Lounge.

Above right: Central atrium.

Left: Exterior of main hall.

Opposite top: Detail of masonry wall.

Opposite: Entrance to wing.

Photography: Robert Polidori, Florian Holzherr.

Skidmore, Owings & Merrill LLP

Greenwich Academy
Upper School & Library
Greenwich, Connecticut

A 23-foot grade dividing the upper and lower levels of Greenwich Academy's 39-acre campus in Greenwich, Connecticut since the independent college preparatory day school for girls was founded in 1827 has finally been bridged. Except that a building—not a bridge—spans the gap. The Patsy G. Howard Upper School & Library, designed by Skidmore, Owings & Merrill, is an award-winning, two-story, 42,000-square-foot classic Modern structure that helps unify the campus while simultaneously providing a luminous environment for 20 classrooms, five science laboratories, student center, visual arts complex, 20,000-volume library with space and technology to serve both the Upper and Middle Schools, and various support spaces and offices. While its massing re-centers the campus on an exterior courtyard, its four interior light chambers act as focal points for the disciplines of science and mathematics, the humanities, the arts and the library. Designed in collaboration withlight artist James Turrell, the glazed chambers flood rooms with natural light by day and dynamic compositions in atmospheric light by night. As Sharon Dietzel, head of Upper School points out, "We have 150 adolescents here, but it's always quiet. All the light has a physical and physiological effect on people. It relaxes them."

Top left: Green roof.
Top right: Courtyard entrance.
Right: Upper school entrance.
Bottom right: Library Interior.
Opposite: Stairway.
Photography: Robert Polidori, Florian Holzherr.

Skidmore, Owings & Merrill LLP

Burr Elementary School
Fairfield, Connecticut

Every school day, 600 fortunate youngsters, grades K-5, enter a heavily wooded forest that, thanks to a new, two-floor, 70,000-square-foot school, seems so close they can practically touch it. Award-winning Burr Elementary School, in Fairfield, Connecticut, whose facilities include classrooms, special science rooms, resource and gifted rooms, music room, library/media center, cafeteria, gymnasium, courtyards and playground, has been designed by Skidmore, Owings & Merrill to celebrate its extraordinary surroundings. Not only does the school's understated concrete and glass exterior blend seamlessly with the site, its interior of white walls, furnishings with wood finishes and natural hues, artificial lighting focused in "patches" to mimic forest light, and movable and reconfigurable equipment do everything possible to bring the forest inside. Innovative floor plans eschew the traditional elementary school typology of double-loaded corridors with special functional elements at either end in favor or classrooms placed along the east and west edges with shared elements in between. To increase light and air, interior courtyards or light wells are located deep within the building's perimeters, sometimes encircling existing trees with their floor-to-ceiling glass walls, to create outdoor classrooms that teachers can use. Burr's principal Gary Kass reports, "It's a nice place to work and learn."

Top right: Lobby and entry court.
Right: Courtyard seen from above.
Bottom left: Arial View
Bottom right: Exterior at Twilight.
Opposite: Corridor
Photography: Robert Polidori, Florian Holzherr.

Skidmore, Owings & Merrill LLP

Brunswick School
Lower School and Gymnasium
Greenwich, Connecticut

Top left: Central atrium.
Left: Gymnasium.
Below left: Library.
Bottom left: Exterior.
Photography: Robert Polidori, Florian Holzherr.

Just why tyrannosaurus rex—or a convincing replica—is cavorting in the atrium of the new Lower School and Gymnasium at the Brunswick School, in Greenwich, Connecticut, is not clear. Nor are two large aquariums in the entrance foyer particularly self-explanatory. But "T-rex" and the fish fit in nicely with the new, three-floor, 50,000-square-foot building, designed by Skidmore, Owings & Merrill, that accommodates students in grades pre-K-4 at the college preparatory day school for boys founded in 1902. The award-winning brick, concrete, glass and wood structure, housing classrooms, library, general assembly room, cafeteria, and multi-purpose room that doubles as gymnasium and theater, draws as much natural light as possible into a learning environment with space for fun as well as scholarship. Having a central atrium with glass walls and skylights in hallways ensures that the Lower School's major public areas are illuminated by daylight, and key functions such as the library, cafeteria, and multi-purpose room are revealed for everyone to see. An exterior embodying a contemporary vision of academic architecture, accompanied by interiors outfitted in transitional furnishings, gives the building an assuring presence on Brunswick's three-part, 118-acre campus where children and a dinosaur can happily work and play.

Stanley Beaman & Sears, Inc.
Architecture and Interiors

135 Walton Street ,NW
Atlanta, GA 30303
404.524.2200
404.524.8610 (Fax)
www.stanleybeamansears.com

Stanley Beaman & Sears, Inc.

Emory University
Winship Cancer Institute
Atlanta, Georgia

Above: Exterior.
Left: Reception.
Opposite: Staircase with inspirational phrases.
Photography: Gary Knight & Associates, Inc.

Cancer strikes people of all walks of life, a point brought home when Robert Woodruff founded the Robert Winship Memorial Clinic at Atlanta's Emory University in 1937. Woodruff, then president of Coca Cola, lost his mother to cancer that year and founded what would become the Winship Cancer Institute in honor of his maternal grandfather. Having occupied various spaces on Emory's 690-acre campus close to downtown Atlanta, the Winship Cancer Institute now

Stanley Beaman & Sears, Inc.

Emory University
Winship Cancer Institute
Atlanta, Georgia

has a splendid new, seven-floor, 280,000-square-foot building of its own, designed by Stanley Beaman & Sears, that actually embeds a visual language of hope, caring and imagination into its details. Modeled in the University's traditional architectural style, the stucco, tile, pre-cast concrete, glass and aluminum-clad Winship Cancer Institute contrasts with typical research facilities by placing researchers, who normally surround themselves with an academic setting, in contemporary, state-of-the-art interiors where they enjoy regular and informal contact with clinicians involved in patient care. Thus, four floors of diagnostic and clinic space, featuring oncology clinics, 80-station infusion center, and patient/family amenities in a patient-friendly healing environment, are combined with three floors of research laboratories, laboratory support, and offices, accompanied by a conference center, faculty support, and public space, to give the Institute its unique character. The uplifting nature of the award-winning design, highlighted by an illuminated entry tower, monumental staircase, and inspirational phrases woven

into the interior design, actually began with its planning, when the design team confronted and resolved such issues as a tight site almost entirely surrounded by other buildings, a complex array of underground utilities, a demanding, fast-track schedule, and a stringent budget. Commenting on the successful completion of the Institute's latest home, Charles T. Andrews, senior associate vice president for space planning and construction at the University, declares, "During Stanley Beaman & Sears's work on this project, their team performance has been outstanding. They have exhibited a real customer attitude and patient focus, and have told us on more than one occasion that they will 'do whatever it takes' to make this project a success. They have delivered on their promises."

Below left: Corridor on research floor.
Below right: Entry tower.
Bottom left: Staircase and elevator bank.
Bottom right: Staircase landing.
Opposite: Laboratory.
Photography: Gary Knight & Associates, Inc.

Stanley Beaman & Sears, Inc.

North Georgia College & State University
Health & Natural Science Center
Dahlonega, Georgia

A proud tradition as Georgia's second oldest public institution of higher education, founded in 1873, and the state's first coeducational college doesn't deter North Georgia College & State University from being a forward looking institution—even as it cherishes its role as one of the nation's six senior military colleges. Visible proof of its progressive outlook is not hard to find on the 112-acre campus in Dahlonega, an historic community in the Blue Ridge Mountains where America's first gold rush took place in 1828. The new, four-story, 120,000-square-foot Health & Natural Science Center, designed by Stanley Beaman & Sears, is a bold, contemporary building of brick and glass that eloquently conveys the infinite dimensions of learning through such elements as its glazed lobby/entrance atrium, featuring an exhibit wall, a sharply canted curtain wall that alludes to the mineshafts of Dahlonega's gold rush days, and a catwalk

Top: Exterior at twilight.

Above left: Fourth floor view of atrium.

Above right: Planetarium.

Opposite: Exterior at dusk.

Photography: Jim Roof Creative Photography.

206

Stanley Beaman & Sears, Inc.

North Georgia College & State University
Health & Natural Science Center
Dahlonega, Georgia

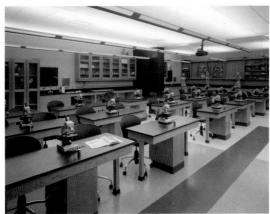

lining the window wall, and its sharply angled masses. Yet the award-winning building is also an effective, state-of-the-art learning environment. Its large wing focuses on the needs of the school with classrooms, laboratories, offices of the nursing, physical therapy and biology departments, and a small primary-care clinic on the first-floor, run by the nursing and physical therapy departments. By contrast, its small wing is the more public part of the facility, offering a 350-seat lecture hall, a planetarium, and such shared spaces as a media center/library and computer laboratories. If the construction testifies to the close working relationship established between the faculty and the design team, the University could not be more pleased. "All my expectations of a business relationship were surpassed and my paradigm completely updated," observes Dr. Robert J. Laird, chair of the physical therapy department. "The efforts of the SBS team spoke volumes about pride, integrity and customer satisfaction."

Top left: Atrium seen from catwalk.

Top right: Main entrance.

Above left: Biology lab.

Photography: Jim Roof Creative Photography.

208

Thompson, Ventulett, Stainback & Associates (TVS)

2700 Promenade Two
1230 Peachtree Steet NE
Atlanta, GA 30309
404.888.6600
404.888.6700 (Fax)
www.tvsa.com

Thompson, Ventulett, Stainback & Associates (TVS)

Thompson, Ventulett, Stainback & Associates (TVS)

Agnes Scott College
McCain Library
Decatur, Georgia

Of course it looks magnificent—but does it compute? The look remains Collegiate Gothic at Agnes Scott College's McCain Library, a stately limestone and brick structure originally completed in 1936 on the central quadrangle of the school's 100-acre campus in Decatur, Georgia. However, thanks to a comprehensive, 70,000-square-foot renovation and expansion designed by Thompson, Ventulett, Stainback & Associates in association with Perry, Dean, Rogers & Partners, the building now boasts new media technolo-

gies along with multi-media classrooms and study and reading spaces for individual and group use. Much of the original structure has been meticulously preserved, including the west façade lining the quadrangle, the vaulted main reading room, and a former garden that is now a landscaped courtyard. By contrast, the new wing uses contemporary architecture to honor the past without mimicking it—highlighted by generous glazing and high-tech metal sunscreens on the south façade—and to nearly double the existing

floor area. Yet there's no doubt that the renewal of the McCain Library and the addition of the Alston Campus Center, created by the same design team, give this independent liberal arts college for women a corridor of activity that is entirely new yet wholly in keeping with its 117-year-old tradition.

Top left: Lowers reading room.
Top right: Exterior.
Right: Stack in original structare.
Opposite: Main reading room.
Photography: Brian Gassel/TVS.

210

Thompson, Ventulett, Stainback & Associates (TVS)

Florida Community College at Jacksonville
Nathan H. Wilson Center for the Arts
Jacksonville, Florida

Top right: Lobby.
Right: Entry.
Opposite left: Exterior.
Opposite right: Art gallery.
Opposite: Performance hall.
Photography: Brian Gassel/TVS.

It's not just stagecraft to say the curtain rises on the South Campus of Florida Community College at Jacksonville with its new, two-story, 136,000-square-foot Nathan H. Wilson Center for the Arts, a four-building complex designed by Thompson, Ventulett, Stainback & Associates in association with Saxelby, Powell, Roberts & Ponder. South Campus is the home of the College's art, music and theater programs, and the modern brick, metal and glass-clad Wilson Center, comprising a 530-seat proscenium theater, 185-seat black box theater, art gallery, lobby, conference center, music studios, acoustically advanced music suites, recording laboratories, classrooms, rehearsal spaces, dressing rooms and support spaces. All of this stands beside a lake at the entrance to the campus as a dramatic invitation to students, faculty and visitors alike. Thanks to close collaboration between the school's faculty and the design team, the Wilson Center enables the College to offer students a program of professional quality rarely achieved in academia. As an added benefit, the Wilson Center's cantilevered, covered entry welcomes the College's approximately 20,800 students, matriculating at the two-year institution's five campuses and seven academic centers, as well as the residents of greater Jacksonville, to a splendid new venue for the arts.

Thompson, Ventulett, Stainback & Associates (TVS)

University of Georgia
Performing and Visual Arts Complex
Athens, Georgia

Like a small city, the University of Georgia, established as America's first state-chartered university in 1785, shelters 33,456 students on a 605-acre main campus in Athens, some 60 miles northeast of Atlanta, and other locations. Unlike most cities of comparable size, the University has developed an ambitious, new, 600,000-square-foot Performing and Visual Arts Complex, designed by Thompson, Ventulett, Stainback & Associates in association with Craig, Gaulden & Davis, to bolster its commitment to education in the arts and stand as a gateway to its new, 75-acre East Campus. The Arts Complex represents a community of five buildings on the shoulder of a hilltop, organized around a new green quadrangle, in ac-

cordance with a master plan also developed by Thompson, Ventulett, Stainback & Associates. The two performance spaces within the recently completed, 199,275-square-foot Performing Arts Center, 1,100-seat Hugh Hodgson Concert Hall and 360-seat Ramsey Concert Hall, have promptly demonstrated their value to the school, community and music lovers everywhere through superb acoustics and clear sightlines. Yoel Levy, music director emeritus of the Atlanta Symphony Orchestra, recently declared, "Hodgson Hall is, by far, the best concert hall in Georgia, and one of the finest in the country."

Thompson, Ventulett, Stainback & Associates (TVS)

Georgia Institute of Technology
Technology Square
Atlanta, Georgia

A long-standing mission to reach across Atlanta's downtown highway connector and touch the midtown business district has become an impressive accomplishment for Georgia Institute of Technology with the inauguration of new, five-building, 1.1 million-square-foot Technology Square on a three-block site previously used as parking lots. Designed by Thompson, Ventulett, Stainback & Associates, the project inserts a dynamic academic community into the heart of downtown, consisting of the College of Management, Global Learning Center, Economic Development Institute, Georgia Tech Foundation, Center for Quality Growth & Regional Development, Georgia Tech Barnes & Noble Bookstore, Georgia Tech Hotel & Conference Center, as well as restaurants, retail shops and parking facilities. While the project focuses primarily on the needs of Georgia Tech and its 17,000 students, it adds a vibrant environment to city life, characterized by bold contemporary architecture, brightly painted courtyards and abundant fenestration. At the project's opening, Atlanta Mayor Shirley Franklin proclaimed, "This is the kind of development that makes the heart and soul of Atlanta. One hundred and eight years ago when Atlanta was the site of the Great Cotton Exposition, this was the kind of development the leaders gathered there had in mind, this kind of synergy and partnership."

Top left: Aerial view.
Top right: Atrium.
Right: Exterior.
Photography: Brian Gassel/TVS.

216

A New Vision

Pass or Fail

By Roger Yee

America's students need all the help they can get to sustain the nation's leadership in the 21st century, and the best new educational facilities reflect their need to succeed

Where were you and what were you doing on October 4, 1957?

Many senior educators will remember. On that day, the Soviet Union launched Sputnik, the world's first space satellite, profoundly humbling the United States. But between the successful orbiting of Explorer I on January 31, 1958 and the first moonwalk by Apollo 11's Neil Armstrong on July 20, 1969, the nation enacted the National Defense Education Act, and American science education went into high gear. Whether or not the No Child Left Behind Act has equal impact in our time, education clearly occupies a pivotal position in maintaining U.S. economic and political leadership. The nation's massive overhaul of its educational facilities, costing roughly $20 billion a year on new construction, expansion and renovation, reflects this concern.

No single incident such as Sputnik triggered America's current concern about its educational system. However, the rapid development of the global economy has given the United States formidable economic rivals. Initially, manufacturing jobs, the unionized, high-paying, blue-collar occupations that ushered millions of Americans into the middle class, began succumbing to foreign competition in the 1970s. Then service jobs, the white-collar occupations expected to fill manufacturing's void, proved susceptible in the 1990s, as

low-cost transportation, reliable communications, and the Internet opened both back-office and R&D opportunities for young, well-educated and low-paid workers overseas.

Should America's educational system be the whipping boy for weakness in its economy? The dilemmas besetting such basic U.S. industries as automobile manufacturing are at least their own fault. Yet the nation's schools do prepare young people for the workplace, where the quality of their education has raised serious questions.

Is mediocrity the American way?

Signs of trouble are not hard to find in America's sprawling and heterogeneous public and private educational systems. Regular surveys of grade school students through the U.S. Department of Education's National Assessment of Educational Progress, known as "the nation's report card," show that public, private, charter and religious schools all suffer from wide fluctuations in quality and effectiveness, and children's well-publicized

Project shown: Kohl's Children's Museum, Glenview, Illinois, Booth Hansen, architect.

struggles to gain proficiency in reading and mathematics are far from over. In reading, 31 percent of fourth-graders and 32 percent of eighth-graders performed at or above the proficiency level in 2003. In mathematics, 32 percent of fourth-graders and 29 percent of eighth-graders performed at or above the proficiency level in 2003.

Comparing American students with their foreign counterparts produces equally problematic results. In the Program for International Student Assessment conducted by the Organization for Economic Cooperation and Development (OECD), which measures 15-year-olds' capabilities in reading literacy, mathematics literacy and science literacy every three years, students from other nations outperform Americans in all three categories. In reading literacy, the U.S. average score was not measurably different from the OECD average in 2003. In mathematics literacy, the U.S. average score was below the OECD average in 2003 and far behind such leaders as Japan, Korea, and New Zealand. In science literacy, the U.S. average score was below the OECD average in 2003 and behind such leaders as Korea, Japan and Finland.

Other anecdotal evidence strongly suggests that American schools and the students they prepare for the adult world must raise the quality of teachers, academic standards and educational facilities without letting costs get out of control.

• The dropout rate for high school students stands at approximately 30 percent. For Latinos and African Americans, disproportionately burdened with poverty and illness, the rate approaches 50 percent.

• Top students rarely consider teaching careers, partly because stifling bureaucracy smothers individual initiative, and partly because

teachers are persistently underpaid. Salaries ranged from a low of $33,236 in South Dakota to a high of $56,516 in Connecticut in 2003-2004, according to the American Federation of Teachers.

• Rising costs for tuition, fees, room and board are pricing private colleges and universities (averaging $30,367 in 2006) beyond the reach of middle-income families and discouraging lower-income families from applying at all. Worse, as more students turn to public schools because of their affordability (averaging $12,796 in 2006), these institutions must compensate for reduced public funding by obliging their families to cover the shortfall. Paradoxi-

cally, real earnings for college graduates without advanced degrees have fallen five years in a row, but the cost of college has soared by 63 percent at public schools and 47 percent at private schools over the last 15 years.

• A broad decline in U.S. science achievement, as measured by the percentage the nation spends on basic research, the numbers of patent grants and articles published in scientific and engineering journals, and the percentage of 24-year-olds with science degrees, is threatening America's half-century of eminence in science and technology. Educators note that almost 40 percent of new graduate students in science and engineering are foreign students with temporary visas.

An "A" for architectural improvement

Fortunately, there is more than a glimmer of light at the end of the school corridor. Working closely with educators, students, families and communities, architects and interior designers are addressing issues where coordinating educational practice and environmental design can produce real synergy. To cite but a few educational concepts that designers have effectively translated into spatial concepts in recent years: students do not all learn in the same way; smaller classes and smaller schools help students succeed; younger students benefit from a separate environment away from older students; improving environmental conditions can raise academic performance and let buildings operate year round; schools and communities both gain through shared

Projects shown (left to right, top to bottom): Pennsylvania State University, Eastview Terrace, State College, Pennsylvania, CBT, architect; Oberlin College, Science Center, Oberlin, Ohio, Payette, architect; Blythewood High School, Blythewood, South Carolina, Perkins & Will, architect; Florida Community College at Jacksonville, Nathan H. Wilson Center for the Arts, Jacksonville, Florida, Thompson, Ventulett, Stainback & Associates, architect.

emeco
THE ALUMINUM CHAIR COMPANY

THE AUTHENTIC 1006 NAVY® CHAIR.   MADE IN AMERICA.   GUARANTEED FOR LIFE.   PHONE 1 717 637 5951   WWW.EMECO.NET

Built of 80% recycled aluminum, 40% post consumer content, Emeco chairs and stools contribute to LEED™ credit #4.2 Recycled Content.

facilities; and social interaction is a vital component of education. Obviously, no single improvement in school design will galvanize education overnight. As the New York Times noted in a July 19, 2006 editorial, "Public vs. Private Schools," there is little mystery about what distinguishes superior schools from failing ones: good

• Unaccustomed as educators are to cooperating with community groups to share facilities, successful joint efforts involving school libraries, gymnasiums, cafeterias and the like show that these partnerships can bolster public support for school construction.

teachers, high standards and involved parents. Yet improvements in school design that directly support teachers and students can be surprisingly effective. Consider these examples.

• Making classrooms and other facilities more flexible gives teachers latitude to engage students through multiple learning styles, since their floor plans accept many configurations for students, equipment and activities.

• Multiple-use spaces are being developed to stretch budgets by letting one facility—"cafetoriums" are commonplace—serve two or more functions that might otherwise exceed construction budgets.

• When smaller classes and smaller schools are not always financially feasible, large schools can be built using smaller components that maintain some autonomy. This is particularly applicable where students in a school's upper and lower grades would be better off physically separated.

• Student lounges, atriums and corridors with seating nooks reassure students that social interaction during the academic day is encouraged.

A fascinating trend in educational facility design is now unfolding on the nation's college and university campuses, where educators are focusing on improving the quality of campus life. Concerned that the Internet, a battery of electronic gadgets and personal comforts, and lingering emotional immaturity are aggravating student alienation, causing students to fail, and endangering the community-oriented way of life on campus—and backed by studies showing that the sooner students become socially comfortable on campus, the more likely they are to adopt the broad imperatives of attending college—institutions are turning to architects, interior designers and planners to give campuses venues for socializing and community activity. The results are showing up everywhere.

• Dormitories now offer strategically placed and attractive entry lobbies, lounges, laundries, study rooms and cafés to give students informal opportunities for socialization.

• Student centers are opening with facilities for individual and group activity, including lounges, cafés, retail shops, study areas, office space and entertainment venues, welcoming students, parents and alumni alike.

• Libraries increasingly incorporate such facilities as classrooms, seminar rooms, study spaces and cafés, where group activity and conversation are encouraged, along with new media to reflect changing ways of conducting research and study.

• Dining halls have abandoned traditional serving lines for marketplace-style serving stations, innovative fare, and seating at tables, booths and lounge settings, to make dining more pleasurable and social.

• Recreation centers acknowledge the desire for recreation and fitness among students who are not varsity athletes by offering a variety of facilities, organized activities, state-of-the-art equipment, and professional training and counseling.

Projects shown (left to right, top to bottom): University of California, Davis, Tercero Dining Commons, Davis, California, BAR Architects, architect; The School of the Art Institute of Chicago, 162 North State Street Residences, Chicago, Illinois, Booth Hansen, architect; Vanderbilt University, Eskind Biomedical Research Library, Nashville, Tennessee, Davis Brody Bond-Aedas, architect; Lawrence Technical University, University Technology and Learning Complex, Southfield, Michigan, Gwathmey Siegel & Associates, Architects, LLC, architect.

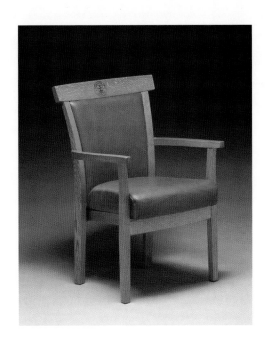

Beeken Parsons

REAL WOOD   REAL·JOINTS   REAL CRAFTSMANSHIP   REAL VALUE

1611 Harbor Road at Shelburne Farms   Shelburne, VT   05482
www.beekenparsons.com   802.985.2913   info@beekenparsons.com

FSC
FSC Supplier

• Many institutions are embracing LEED (Leadership in Energy and Environmental Design) certification by the U.S. Green Building Council and other comparable measures to promote construction incorporating health benefits for occupants and neighbors.

• Campus grounds now cultivate landscapes with generous pedestrian paths, focal points such as fountains, sculpture and outdoor gathering spaces, and vehicular roads and parking lots relocated to peripheral areas to make walking safer and more appealing.

Design on the academic frontline

Are design projects meant to improve student life on college and university campuses actually fulfilling their promises? To address this question first-hand, five respected architecture firms and schools they are currently serving have generously shared their experiences with Educational Environments No. 3. Commenting on their projects are CBT Architects and Pennsylvania State University; BAR Architects and the University of California, Davis; Booth Hansen and the School of the Art Institute of Chicago; Thompson Ventulett Stainback Architects and Florida Community College; and Sasaki Associates and Bates College.

Eastview Terrace at Pennsylvania State University:
See and be seen.
Even as Pennsylvania State University's new 811-bed, seven-building residential complex for upper classmen, Eastview Terrace,

began rising on the State College campus, Christopher Hill, AIA, a design principal and student housing expert at CBT, the facility's architect, continued to evaluate its innovations. "We gave everyone relatively small single rooms and single baths to draw them out into the semi-private and public spaces just outside their doors," Hill recalls. "But we still wondered, 'If we build it, will they come?'" He needn't have worried. Eastview Terrace has a long waiting list. What appeals to juniors and seniors, according to Sandy Harpster, PSU's director of housing, is the low-rise facility's intimately scaled blend of privacy, which they value highly, and relaxed, "see and be seen" social setting. Indoors, open suites of eight to sixteen singles share living rooms/lounges and kitchenettes. Outdoors, small courtyards nurture a residential ambiance. All this makes Eastview Terrace an attractive alternative to off-campus housing. "You can enjoy as much privacy and interaction as you want," Harpster notes. "It's our most expensive campus housing, but students really like it."

Tercero Dining Commons at the University of California, Davis:
Even the chancellor dines here.
Tercero Dining Commons at the University of California, Davis, has been around long enough to see its brutalist concrete structure change from "fresh" and "bold" to "dreary" and "institutional." However, with more students on the way, BAR Architects has profoundly changed it, transforming the dining experience and adding new spaces for socializing, counseling, tutoring, recreation and seminars. "We brought coherence and scale to the exterior," states Michael Reid, a senior associate of BAR Architects. "For the interiors, we took sunlight deep inside, introduced better circulation, and created spaces that are fun and inviting without being Disneyfied." The traditional servery and dining hall, for example, have yielded to marketplace-style serving platforms and distinct dining areas offering a wealth of choices. "Not only do Tercero's 2,400 students like the new arrangement and spend more time here," declares Kate Scott, UCD's director of design services for the Division of Student Affairs, "the staff is happier out in the open, where they can greet students and show off their skills." Actually, faculty members and the chancellor are showing up too.

Learn Well.

162 North State Street at the School of the Art Institute of Chicago: *No campus, no problem!*

For an institution of higher education lacking a campus, the School of the Art Institute of Chicago closely monitors the de facto campus surrounding it: Chicago's historic "Loop," where four other schools maintain facilities. SAIC's need to provide housing and studios for first- and second-year art students has produced a lively, 500-bed, 17-story student residence, 162 North State Street, designed by Booth Hansen. The building simultaneously honors Chicago architecture and respects its independent-minded students. "Our design picks up such historic themes as bay windows and projecting cornices," observes Laurence Booth, FAIA, design principal of Booth Hansen. "But it's also rugged and practical, so students can get dirty, make noise and pin things on walls." Tony Smith, president of SAIC, praises the dormitory's pioneering spirit. "Art students are highly focused and don't want meal plans or the traditional trappings of college life," he reports. "They appreciate what the building gives them to cope with city life, including the lounges, kitchens, exercise room and laundry, and they spend hours in the studios." It's a popular dormitory—for students who don't want one.

Nathan H. Wilson Center for the Arts at Florida Community College: *Let the show go on.*

Community colleges enable students to attend college near home, minimize expenses and hold jobs. But pragmatism exacts a price. To quote Dr. Earl Farris, emeritus dean of the humanities and arts for Florida Community College at Jacksonville, "There's no campus life when you go directly from classes to work." Fortunately, the new Nathan H. Wilson Center for the Arts, designed by Thompson Ventulett Stainback & Associates, cultivates close ties with regional arts organizations to enhance campus and community life. This four-building, 136,000-square-foot complex houses art, music and theater facilities on FCCJ's South Campus, reinforcing its established role in arts training. Visitors can't miss it. "The Center stands beside the entrance to the campus," indicates Robert Balke, AIA, LEED AP, a principal of TVSA, "projecting a new, positive image." Better yet, it forms partnerships with performing arts companies to use such facilities as its 530-seat proscenium theater and 185-seat black box theater, so students can participate in professional productions. "You won't find training like this anywhere else locally," Dr. Farris concludes. "The Center benefits students and Jacksonville alike."

Dining Commons at Bates College:

Where everyone connects.

Admired for its academic programs, Bates College is earnestly de-

veloping new facilities to enhance student life on campus in Lewiston, Maine. "Student life is a constant topic here," agrees Steve Sawyer, the school's associate dean of students. A cornerstone of Bates's master plan is the new 750-seat, 60,000-square-foot Dining Commons, designed by Sasaki Associates. "The Commons reflects Bates's uniquely egalitarian culture," reports Alan Resnick, AIA, LEED AP, Sasaki's principal in charge. Its opening in 2008 introduces marketplace-style serving stations and spacious dining areas, along with a fireplace lounge, retail market, and meeting spaces for students, faculty, staff and alumni. Since Lewiston has few commercial attractions for students, the Commons will be a major destination. "Many groups participated in the planning," says Robert Bremm, Bates's director of physical plant. "We received helpful comments, and everyone bought into the design." The increased interaction expected between staff and students is universally welcomed. "Students like discussing what's for dinner with the people preparing it," explains Erin Foster Zsiga, assistant dean of students and director of student housing at Bates. "Our staff is like family." And the Commons will feel like home.

As these narratives demonstrate, educational facilities can actively support the learning experiences of students and teachers in countless ways. However, good schools still start with good teachers, high academic standards, and motivated communities of students, families and public-spirited citizens. If the United States wants to prevail in the global challenges it faces, it will treat education as a critical investment in its own future, and recognize an effective educational environment as a fair down payment for continued leadership of the free world.

Projects shown (left to right, top to bottom): The Spence School, New York, New York, FXFOWLE Architects, PC, architect; Bates College, Dining Commons, Lewiston, Maine, Sasaki Associates, Inc., architect; Erie High School, Erie, Colorado, H+L Architecture, architect; Vanderbilt University, Sarratt Student Center, Nashville, Tennessee, Bruner Cott, architect.

Building World Class Educational Environments

From concept to completion, Audio Visual Innovations works closely with architects, designers, facilities managers and both IT and construction professionals, to design, build and install world-class audiovisual environments for all forms of presentation, communication and collaboration. Combining our expertise with state-of-the-art equipment, we deliver the complete integrated audiovisual solution with attention to the design details of your classroom, training room or auditorium.

Since 1979, we have been providing custom solutions which allow you to energize and motivate learning. Let the experts at AVI help you in customizing your next multimedia technology space. To discuss your specific needs with an AVI representative, give us a call at **1-800-282-6733.**

Audio Visual® Innovations
Your Source For Being Seen And Heard.

DESIGN • BUILD • INSTALL | 1-800-282-6733 • www.aviinc.com

Resources*

Agnes Scott College, McCain Library
Design Firm: Thompson, Ventulett, Stainback & Associates
Furniture: David Edwards, Geiger, Howe, Keilhauer, Thomas Moser
Carpets & Flooring: Crab Orchard Stone
Lighting: Hubbarton Forge
Window Treatments: Vimco Roller Shades
General Contractors: Beers/Skahska
Lighting Consultants: Ramon Hoya

Agnes Scott College, Wallace M. Alston Campus Center
Design Firm: Thompson, Ventulett, Stainback & Associates
Furniture: Leland International, Martin Brattrud, Vecta
Carpets & Flooring: Armstrong, Constantine, Forbo, Shaw
Lighting: Ardec, Bronzolite, Focal Point, Hess, Lightolier, Lite Control, McPhilben, SPI, Visa
Ceilings: Hunter Douglas, USG
Window Treatments: Construction Specialties, Graham Windows, Jonquil Steel
General Contractors: Beers Construction Company
Lighting Consultants: Ramon Luminance Design

Baltimore School for the Arts
Design Firm: Cho Benn Holback & Associates
Furniture: American Office Interiors
Carpets & Flooring: Armstrong, Atlas, Harlequin, Maucau Tile, Mondo
Fabrics: Decoustics
Lighting: Neoray, Prudential, RSA Lighting, Winona
Wallcoverings and Paint: Sherwin Williams
Window Treatments: Bau Contract
General Contractors: Whiting Turner/Banks Contracting
Lighting Consultants: Hilman DiBernardo Leiter Castell

Blythewood High School, Richland School District Two
Design Firm: Perkins+Will
Furniture: KI
Carpets & Flooring: Armstrong, David Allen Sports, Mondo/Connor, Shaw
Lighting: Lithonia
Ceilings: Celotex

Wallcoverings and Paint: Sherwin Williams
Window Treatments: Bali
General Contractors: Southern Management Group

Brandeis University, Lemberg Center
Design Firm: CBT
Lighting: Lithonia, Prescolite
Ceilings: Armstrong
Wallcoverings and Paint: Jhane Barnes Textiles, Sherwin Williams
General Contractors: John Moriarty & Associates, Inc.
Lighting Consultants: Sladen Feinstein Integrateddd Lighting, Inc.

Brunswick School, Lower School & Gymnasium
Design Firm: Skidmore, Owings & Merrill, LLP
Furniture: Legere Group Ltd., Unadilla
Carpets & Flooring: Shaw
Lighting: Color Kinetics, Erco, I-Light, Neoray
Ceilings: Armstrong
Wallcoverings and Paint: Benjamin Moore, Forbo
Window Treatments: MechoShade
General Contractors: Turner Construction

Burr Elementary School
Design Firm: Skidmore, Owings & Merrill, LLP
Furniture: Columbia
Carpets & Flooring: Armstrong, Karastan, Robbins
Fabrics: Dazian
Lighting: Metalux
Ceilings: Armstrong
Wallcoverings and Paint: Benjamin Moore, Forbo
Window Treatments: MechoShade
General Contractors: Turner Construction

The Calhoun School
Design Firm: FXFOWLE Architects
Furniture: Figueras International Seating, Nuovo
Carpets & Flooring: Armstrong, Azrock, Interface, Johnsonite, Lonseal, Roppe, Shaw
Lighting: Alco, At-Lite, Belfer, Columbia, Edison Price, Illuminating Experiences, Legion, Lightolier, Luce Plan, Mark Lighting, Prescolite, Winona
Wallcoverings and Paint: Benjamin Moore, Daltile, Forbo

California State University, Fullerton, Kinesiology and Health Science Building
Design Firm: HMC Architects
Carpets & Flooring: Armstrong, Burke, Daltile
Wallcoverings and Paint: Dunn Edwards, Vista
General Contractors: Swinerton Builders

Carnegie Institution of Washington, Global Ecology Research Center
Design Firm: EHDD Architecture
Furniture: Steelcase
Carpets & Flooring: Armstrong, Davis Colors, Interface
Lighting: Lightolier, Sistemawx, Zumtobel
Ceilings: Armstrong
Wallcoverings and Paint: Benjamin Moore, Frazee
Window Treatments: MechoShade
General Contractors: DPR Construction, Inc.
Lighting Consultants: JS Nolan + Associates

Chester Union Free Middle/Senior High School
Design Firm: Cannon Design
Furniture: Allsteel, Community, KI, OFS, Peter Pepper, Sit-On-It, Versteel, Wenger
Carpets & Flooring: Azrock, Daltile, Olympia, Shaw-Prince Street
Fabrics: Momentum
Ceilings: USG
Wallcoverings and Paint: Benjamin Moore, Sherwin Williams
Window Treatments: MechoShade
General Contractors: RBL Construction

College of Wooster, Henry Luce III Residence Hall
Design Firm: Dagit Saylor Architects
General Contractors: Bogner Construction Co.

Cornwall Central High School
Design Firm: Cannon Design
Furniture: Allsteel, Hon, Inwood, KI, Krug, Sico, Sit-On-It, Smith Systems, Vecta, Versteel, Wenger
Carpets & Flooring: Armstrong, Bentley, Crossville, Daltile, Dec-O-Tex, Designweave, General Polymers, Interface
Fabrics: Momentum
Ceilings: Ceilings Plus, Ecophon, USG
Wallcoverings and Paint: JM Lynne, Sherwin Williams, Wolf Gordon

Lincoln County High School, Hamlin, West Virginia
ZMM, Inc. Architects & Engineers

Creating better environments

Sustainable development
Taking care of the environment

MARMOLEUM®
ARTOLEUM®   forbo

*For more information on
Forbo's commitment to the
environment, please call
1-800-842-7839
for a copy of Forbo's new
"Taking care of the
environment" brochure.*

Environmental responsibility is a core value of Forbo, and has been for decades. Forbo is the world leader in linoleum, and its global brand, Marmoleum, is associated with beautiful design, durability, dependability, and sustainability.

Marmoleum gets a great start from nature, which provides renewable raw materials that require little energy to harvest, extract, and process. Excellence in environmental performance is achieved, however, through highly efficient and rigorously controlled manufacturing processes. This is fully transparent to the market through our publicly available third-party, peer-reviewed full LCA (Life Cycle Assessment) study.

Forbo continually strives to improve the performance of Marmoleum, and is pleased to introduce Topshield, an innovative water-based finish that considerably reduces the need for initial maintenance and chemicals, while providing lower cleaning costs and a better long term appearance retention than any other resilient flooring.

At the end of its long, useful life, Marmoleum is fully biodegradable. From the indoor environment to the natural environment, Forbo's products and services combine design and functionality to create better environments.

MARMOLEUM®
with **topshield**™

T: 1-800-842-7839
info@fL-NA.com
www.forboflooringna.com

creating better environments

Window Treatments: MechoShade
General Contractors: JMOA Engineers PC

Deerfield Academy, Koch Center for Science, Math & Technology
Design Firm: Skidmore, Owings & Merrill, LLP
Furniture: Legere Group Ltd., Vecta, Vitra
Carpets & Flooring: Karastan
Fabrics: Acoustical Solutions, Maharam
Lighting: Selux
Ceilings: Artisan Sound Control
Wallcoverings and Paint: Benjamin Moore
Window Treatments: MechoShade
Lighting Consultants: James Turrell

Dillard University, DUICEF Building
Design Firm: Davis Brody Bond-Aedas
Furniture: KI, Lectun Hall Seating
Carpets & Flooring: Mohawk
Ceilings: Armstrong
Wallcoverings and Paint: Sherwin Williams
Window Treatments: MechoShade
General Contractors: Carl E. Woodward,LLC
Lighting Consultants: Associated Design Group

Erie High School
Design Firm: H + L Architecture
Carpets & Flooring: Armstrong, Collins & Aikman, Forbo
Ceilings: Celotex
Wallcoverings and Paint: Sherwin Williams
General Contractors: Adolfson & Peterson Construction

Georgia Institute of Technology, Technology Square
Design Firm: Thompson, Ventulett, Stainback & Associates
Furniture: Teknion
Carpets & Flooring: Interface, Lees, Shaw
Lighting: Focal Point, Hightower
Ceilings: Armstrong
Wallcoverings and Paint: Koroseal, Sherwin Williams
Window Treatments: Levolor, MechoShade
General Contractors: Holder/Hardin Construction
Lighting Consultants: Paul Helms Lighting Design

Greenwich Academy, Upper School & Library
Design Firm: Skidmore, Owings & Merrill, LLP
Furniture: Davis
Carpets & Flooring: Karastan
Lighting: Zumtobel
Ceilings: Armstrong
Wallcoverings and Paint: Benjamin Moore
Window Treatments: Solar Shade
General Contractors: Turner Construction
Lighting Consultants: James Turrell

Harvard University, Harvard Dance Center
Design Firm: Bruner/Cott
Furniture: Hussey Seating
Carpets & Flooring: Decathlon, Forbo, Harlequin, Masland
Lighting: Lightolier
Wallcoverings and Paint: Decoustics, Guilford of Maine, ICI
Window Treatments: Hunter Douglas
General Contractors: Consigli Construction Co. Inc.
Lighting Consultants: Light This

Harvard University, University Hall
Design Firm: Bruner/Cott
Carpets & Flooring: Marmoleum, Persian (antique) carpets
Lighting: Elliptipar
Wallcoverings and Paint: Benjamin Moore
Window Treatments: MechoShade
General Contractors: Shawmut Design & Construction

James Madison School of Excellence
Design Firm: Cannon Design
Furniture: American Seating, Buffalo Hotel Supply, Monroe Kitchen Equipment
Carpets & Flooring: Collins & Aikman, Mannington, Robbins
Lighting: Daybright, Emergi-Lite, Lightolier
Ceilings: Daltile
Wallcoverings and Paint: Sherwin Williams

King/Robinson Magnet School
Design Firm: Davis Brody Bond-Aedas
Carpets & Flooring: Armstrong, DalTile, Dupont, Shaw
Lighting: Edison Price, Elliptipar, Lightolier, Lithonia, Louis Poulsen, Luceplan, Metalux
Ceilings: Armstrong, Hunter Douglas

Wallcoverings and Paint: Sherwin Williams
General Contractors: Kanover Construction Corporation with C&R Development Co.,Inc.
Lighting Consultants: Fisher Marantz Stone

Kohl Children's Museum
Design Firm: Booth Hansen
Carpets & Flooring: Interface, Marmoleum
Lighting: Times Square
Ceilings: USG
Wallcoverings and Paint: Sherwin Williams
Window Treatments: Kawneer
General Contractors: Pepper Construction
Lighting Consultants: Schuler & Shook

Lawrence Technological University, University Technology & Learning Complex
Design Firm: Gwathmey Siegel & Associates Architects, llc
Carpets & Flooring: Armstrong, Daltile
Ceilings: USG
Wallcoverings and Paint: Techwall
Window Treatments: Levolor, MechoShade
General Contractors: Barton Malow Company
Lighting Consultants: Hillmann, Di Bernardo, Leither & Castelli

Lehigh University, Zoellner Performing Arts Center
Design Firm: Dagit Saylor Architects
General Contractors: Alvin H. Butz, Inc.
Lighting Consultants: Design Collaborative

Messiah College, Larsen Student Union
Design Firm: Cho Benn Holback & Associates
Carpets & Flooring: Crossville, Mohawk
Fabrics: ArcCom, Maharam
Lighting: Cooper, Eureka, Lightolier, Winona
Ceilings: Ecophon, Rulon
Wallcoverings and Paint: Duron Paint, Novawall
Window Treatments: Wausau
General Contractors: R.S. Mowery and Sons, Inc.
Lighting Consultants: The Lighting Practice, Inc.
Kitchen Consultants: H. David Porter Associates, Inc.

Middlebury College, Middlebury College Library
Design Firm: Gwathmey Siegel & Associates Architects, llc
Furniture: Beeken Parsons
Carpets & Flooring: Diversified Interiors, Inc.

Makes style and maintenance
ELEMENTARY.

evolvingstyles

SMOOTH RUBBER TILE & SHEET

Now you can design your high-traffic areas with a steady diet of style, yet still give them the durability and resilience to stand tall against daily wear-and-tear. That's Evolving Styles. Whatever life throws at it, Evolving Styles eats it up with minimal maintenance for a look that stays true from one day to the next.

Call us today for more information:
1.800.633.3151   www.flexcofloors.com

FLEXCO®

innovative design. flooring performance.

Fabrics: Architectural Design Resources
Ceilings: Advanced Ceiling Systems
Wallcoverings and Paint: Russ/Wood Decorating, Inc.
Window Treatments: Marietta Drapery & Window
General Contractors: Lee Kennedy Company Inc.
Lighting Consultants: Hillman DeBernardo & Associates

Moraine Valley Community College
Design Firm: Booth Hansen
Window Treatments: Hertz
Lighting Consultants: Schuler & Shook

New Jersey Institute of Technology, Campus Center & Academic Building
Design Firm: Gwathmey Siegel & Associates Architects, llc
General Contractors: Turner Construction
Lighting Consultants: Hillmann, Di Bernardo, Leither & Castelli

The New School, Arnhold Hall, Theresa Lang Cultural Center
Design Firm: FXFOWLE Architects
Furniture: ICF, Knoll
Carpets & Flooring: Monterey
Lighting: Edison Price, Louis Poulsen, TIR Systems
Wallcoverings and Paint: Benjamin Moore, Innovations in Wallcoverings
General Contractors: Corporate Interiors Contracting
Lighting Consultants: Goldstick Lighting Design

Northeastern University, Kerr Hall
Design Firm: Bergmeyer Associates, Inc.
Furniture: A.G.I., Bernhardt, Brandrud, Davis, Helikon, Tuohy
Carpets & Flooring: Lees, Steen-Williams
Fabrics: Knoll, Maharam, Pollack
Lighting: Lightolier
Wallcoverings and Paint: Benjamin Moore

Oberlin College, Science Center
Design Firm: Payette
General Contractors: Mosser Construction
Lighting Consultants: Warfel Schrager

Ohio Wesleyan University, ConradesWetherell Science Center
Design Firm: Payette
Fabrics: Knoll
Lighting: Cooper
Ceilings: Armstrong
Window Treatments: MechoShade
General Contractors: Turner Lincoln Construction

Penn State University, Eastview Terrace
Design Firm: CBT/Childs Bertman Tseckares, Inc.
Carpets & Flooring: Shaw
Lighting: Leer Electric
Ceilings: Armstrong
Wallcoverings and Paint: PPG, Saints Painting
Window Treatments: Caldwell
General Contractors: Wyatt Inc.
Lighting Consultants: Brinjac Engineers

Perspectives Charter School
Design Firm: Perkins+Will
Furniture: V/S
Carpets & Flooring: Armstrong
Lighting: Exceline, Lightolier, Prudential
Ceilings: Armstrong
Wallcoverings and Paint: Sherwin Williams
General Contractors: Levine Construction
Lighting Consultants: Perkins+Will

Philadelphia Academy of the Fine Arts, Samuel M.V. Hamilton Building
Design Firm: Dagit Saylor Architects
Furniture: Herman Miller, Knoll, Steelcase, Vitra
Carpets & Flooring: Atlas, Bentley, Daltile
Fabrics: DesignText
Lighting: Artemide, Belfer, Edison Price, Elliptipar, Focal Point, Lite Labs
Ceilings: Ecophon, USG
Wallcoverings and Paint: Maharam, Sherwin Williams
Window Treatments: Pilkington, Traco
General Contractors: Becker & Frondorf
Lighting Consultants: Hefferan Partnership

Pioneer Ridge Elementary School
Design Firm: H + L Architecture
Carpets & Flooring: C+A Maple Flooring Manufacturers Association, Daltile, Johnsonite
Fabrics: KM Fabrics
Lighting: Baselite, Hydrel, Lithonia, Times Square Lighting
Ceilings: USG

Wallcoverings and Paint: National Coatings
Window Treatments: Springs Window Fashions Division
General Contractors: FCI Construction
Lighting Consultants: M.E. Group, Inc.

Randolph-Macon College, Thomas Branch Hall
Design Firm: Glave & Holmes Associates
Furniture: Global Total Office, Mega Office Furniture, National Furniture, Salone, Tolleson, Whitby Delta
Carpets & Flooring: C&A Crossley, Collins & Aikman, Daltile, Forbo, Stone Source
Lighting: Alera, Elliptipar, Prescolite
Wallcoverings and Paint: Benjamin Moore
General Contractors: English Construction Company
Lighting Consultants: Adams & Parnell

Roosevelt University, Ganz Hall
Design Firm: Booth Hansen
Lighting: New Metal Crafts
Wallcoverings and Paint: Chicago Conservation Center (paintings)
General Contractors: Pepper Construction
Lighting Consultants: Schuler & Shook

Salem State College, Peabody & Bowditch Halls
Design Firm: Bergmeyer Associates, Inc.
Furniture: Bright, Carolina, Davis, Lowenstein
Carpets & Flooring: Bentley
Fabrics: Knoll, Maharam
Ceilings: Armstrong
Wallcoverings and Paint: Benjamin Moore

Santee Education Complex
Design Firm: HMC Architects
Carpets & Flooring: Interface, Mannington, Royal Moaa
Ceilings: Armstrong
Wallcoverings and Paint: Benjamin Moore, Dunn Edwards, ICI, Koroseal
Window Treatments: Levolor

The School of the Art Institute of Chicago, 162 North State Street Student Residences
Design Firm: Booth Hansen
Furniture: Michael Heltzer
Carpets & Flooring: Azrock

Society for College and University Planning . . .
Helping You Plan for Higher Education's Future

The Society for College and University Planning (SCUP) is the recognized leader in advancing the knowledge and practice of planning in higher education.

SCUP has nearly 5,000 higher education professionals worldwide interested in planning at all levels and in all contexts. SCUP's mission is to provide higher education professionals with planning knowledge, resources, and connections to achieve institutional goals.

Visit **www.scup.org** for information on how to join this growing community.

If your job involves planning, SCUP can help:

Academic planning
Campus planning
Capital planning
Community relations
Enrollment management
Facility planning
Financial planning
Institutional research planning
IT or technology planning
Master planning
Open spaces
Policy and governance
Space management planning
Strategic planning
Student housing planning
Student services/life planning

Contact SCUP

Contact us at **www.scup.org** for a wealth of frequently updated information and links.

 Society for College and University Planning
339 East Liberty Street • Suite 300
Ann Arbor, Michigan 48104 USA
Phone: 734.998.7832
Fax: 734.998.6532
Email: membership@scup.org

Wallcoverings and Paint: ICI
General Contractors: Wooton Construction
Lighting Consultants: Schuler & Shook

Solana Pacific Elementary School
Design Firm: HMC Architects
Carpets & Flooring: Collins & Aikman
General Contractors: Douglas E. Barnhart
Lighting Consultants: Johnson Consulting
Engineers

The Spence School
Design Firm: FXFOWLE Architects
Carpets & Flooring: Azrock, Shaw
Lighting: Lightolier, Lite Control, Louis Poulsen
Wallcoverings and Paint: Benjamin Moore,
Walltalkers, Zorel
General Contractors: Richter + Ratner
Lighting Consultants: Karen Goldstick and
SBLD Studio

Squashbusters
Design Firm: CBT
Furniture: Epic, Gunlocke, Keilhauer, KI, Metro,
Patrician, Steelcase, Vecta
Carpets & Flooring: American Olean, General
Polymers, Monterey, Shaw
Lighting: Halo
Ceilings: Armstrong, Hunter Douglas, Tectum
Wallcoverings and Paint: ICI Paints
Window Treatments: MechoShade
General Contractors: Shawmut Design &
Construction
Lighting Consultants: Schweppe Lighting &
Design, Inc.

Stephen & Harriet Myers Middle School
Design Firm: Cannon Design
Furniture: AGI, Allsteel, Inwood, KI, Sit-On-It,
Versteel, Wenger
Carpets & Flooring: American Olean, Azrock,
Daltile, Patcraft
Fabrics: Maharam, Momentum, Pallas
Ceilings: Armstrong, Ecophon, USG
Wallcoverings and Paint: Benjamin Moore
Window Treatments: MechoShade

St. Mark's School Center for the Arts
Design Firm: CBT
Furniture: Brayton, Bright, Figueras, Lowenstein,
Wenger

Carpets & Flooring: Atlas, Karastan, Lees
Fabrics: ArcCom, Architex, Edelman Leather,
Momentum, Pallas
Lighting: Baldinger, Custom Metalcraft, Edison
Price, Focal Point, Lightolier, Louis Paulsen
Ceilings: Armstrong
Wallcoverings and Paint: Benjamin Moore, Forbo
Window Treatments: MechoShade, Nysan Shades
General Contractors: Erland Construction, Inc.
Lighting Consultants: Schweppe Lighting &
Design, Inc.

**Syracuse University, Martin J. Whitman
School of Management**
Design Firm: FXFOWLE Architects
Furniture: Clarin, Gunlocke, Haworth, Herman
Miller, KI
Carpets & Flooring: Armstrong, Atlas, Bentley,
Daltile, Dex-O-Tex, Interface, Syracuse Mosaic, Tate
Lighting: Bega, Belfer, Cooper, Edison Price,
ERCO, Focal Point, Gammalux, Linear Lighting,
Litecontrol, Neoray, Prisma, RSA, Wila, Windirect
Wallcoverings and Paint: Sherwin Williams
General Contractors: Hueber-Breuer Construc-
tion Co., Inc.
Lighting Consultants: SBLD Studio

**Towson University, Johnny Unitas Field
House and Sports Complex**
Design Firm: Cho Benn Holback & Associates
Carpets & Flooring: Blueridge Carpet, Tarkett
Lighting: Columbia, Louis Poulsen, Prescolite,
Prudential, Visa
Ceilings: Armstrong
Wallcoverings and Paint: Sherwin Williams
Window Treatments: Levolor, MechoShade
General Contractors: Barton Malow

**Union Theological Seminary & Presbyte-
rian School of Christian Education, William
Smith Morton Library**
Design Firm: Glave & Holmes Associates
Furniture: Century Guild, Ltd.
Carpets & Flooring: Vermont Slate
Lighting: Crenshaw Lighting
Ceilings: Capitol Interiors
Wallcoverings and Paint: TMS
General Contractors: Turner Construction
Company
Lighting Consultants: Renfro Design Group

**University of California, Berkeley, Resi-
dence Halls Units 1 & 2, Infill Student
Housing**
Design Firm: EHDD Architecture
Furniture: August, Inc., DCI Furniture, Howe, KI,
Steelcase, Weiland, West Coast Industries
Carpets & Flooring: Davis Colors, Interface,
Lonseal
Fabrics: Maharam
Lighting: Eliptipar, Prescolite, Shaper Lighting
Ceilings: Armstrong, 3-Form
Wallcoverings and Paint: Frazee, Kelley-Moore
Window Treatments: Graber, Laura Ashley
General Contractors: Rudolph & Stetter, Inc.
Lighting Consultants: Auerbach + Glasan

**University of California, Riverside, Alumni
& Visitors Center**
Design Firm: HMC Architects
Furniture: KI
Carpets & Flooring: Cesar, Daltile, Hanwha L&C
Corp., Mannington
Lighting: Daybrite, Focal Point, Portfolio, Pruden-
tial, Shaper
Ceilings: Armstrong
Wallcoverings and Paint: Benjamin Moore,
Dunn Edwards, ICI Paints, Vista
General Contractors: RC Construction
Lighting Consultants: The Rusika Company

**University of Chicago, Bartlett
Dining Center**
Design Firm: Bruner/Cott
Furniture: Eustis Enterprises, Lombard Chair Co.
Carpets & Flooring: Lees
Lighting: Elliptipar, Kurt Versen, Lightolier, Visa
Ceilings: Armstrong
Wallcoverings and Paint: Sherwin Williams
General Contractors: Pepper Construction Co.
Lighting Consultants: Bruner/Cott & Associates

**University of Cincinnati, Campus Recre-
ation Center**
Design Firm: Morphosis
Furniture: Knoll, Vitra, Willy Guhl
Carpets & Flooring: American Olean, Interface,
Robbins
Ceilings: USG
Wallcoverings and Paint: Eternit, Reynobond

IIDA
INTERNATIONAL INTERIOR DESIGN ASSOCIATION

why iida?

Because while it is all about design, it's also about our Members, professional growth and shaping the future. Take your individual seat and be a part of something greater.

- Opportunities to learn from design leaders.
- Professional networking with over 12,000 Members.
- The chance to shape the future of design through legislative activities.
- Educational opportunities at the Chapter level, including CEUs and NCIDQ prep courses.
- Professional development resources available ONLY to Members.

Visit our website at www.iida.org or call toll free 888.799.IIDA for a membership application today. We're saving you a seat.

The Association for Design Professionals

University of Cincinnati, Tangeman University Center
Design Firm: Gwathmey Siegel & Associates Architects, llc
Furniture: Allermuir, Davis, Keilhauer, Landscape Forms, Lowenstein, Sandler
Carpets & Flooring: Armstrong, J&J Carpet, Mike Carnevale Terrazzo & Tile
Lighting: Legion Lighting, Lithonia, Louis Paulsen, Neoray, RSA Lighting
Ceilings: Armstrong, USG
Wallcoverings and Paint: Sherwin Williams
Window Treatments: MechoShade, Nysan Shades
General Contractors: Reece-Campbell, Inc.
Lighting Consultants: Hillmann, Di Bernardo, Leiter & Castelli

University of Colorado at Colorado Springs, University Center
Design Firm: H + L Architecture
Furniture: Office Specialties
Carpets & Flooring: Atlas, Colorado Hardscapes, Mannington
Lighting: Kim Lighting, Metalumen
Ceilings: Armstrong
Wallcoverings and Paint: Sherwin Williams
General Contractors: M.A. Mortenson

University of Connecticut, Pharmacy/ Biology Building
Design Firm: Davis Brody Bond-Aedas
Furniture: Brayton International, KI, Kusch, Metro, Steelcase, Vecta
Carpets & Flooring: Bentley Prince Street
Fabrics: DesignTex, Luna Textiles, Maharam
Lighting: Alkco, Cooper Lighting, DM Lighting, Fail-Safe, Focal Point, Gammalux, Kurt Versen, Ladolite, Legion, Lightolier, Louis Poulsen, Lucifer, Neoray, Rambusch, RSA, Vibia
Ceilings: Armstrong
Window Treatments: MechoShade
General Contractors: Gilbane Building Company
Lighting Consultants: Thompson + Sears, LLC

University of Denver, Frank H. Ricketson Jr. Law Building
Design Firm: H + L Architecture
Furniture: Brayton, Dauphin, David Edward, Epic, Knoll, Reff, Steelcase, Technion, Versteel
Carpets & Flooring: Atlas, Florbull, Lees, Welsch Quarry
Lighting: Exittorix, Lutron, Neoray, Shaper Lighting, Stemberg Vintage Lighting

Ceilings: Armstrong
Wallcoverings and Paint: Sherwin Williams
General Contractors: Saunders

University of Georgia, Performing and Visual Arts Complex
Design Firm: Thompson, Ventulett, Stainback & Associates
Furniture: Irwin
General Contractors: Brasfield & Gome
Lighting Consultants: Newcomb & Boyd

University of Maryland, Baltimore County, Public Policy Building
Design Firm: Cho Benn Holback & Associates
Carpets & Flooring: Durkan, Karastan
Ceilings: Armstrong, Ecophon
Wallcoverings and Paint: Sherwin Williams
Window Treatments: MechoShade
General Contractors: Whitney-Turner Contracting Co.

University of Maryland, Health Sciences Facility, Phase II
Design Firm: Payette in a joint venture with Design Collective, Inc.
General Contractors: Whiting Turner
Lighting Consultants: Rick Rojas with Steffian Bradley

University of Virginia, Darden School of Business Administration, Sponsors' Hall & Parking Garage
Design Firm: Glave & Holmes Associates
General Contractors: Whiting-Turner Contracting Company

University of Virginia, Peabody Hall
Design Firm: Glave & Holmes Associates
Carpets & Flooring: Costen Floor, Durkan, Shaw
Lighting: Brass Light Gallery
General Contractors: Martin/Horn Contractors

Vanderbilt University, Eskind Biomedical Research Library
Design Firm: Davis Brody Bond-Aedas
Furniture: Bernhardt, Knoll
Carpets & Flooring: Armstrong, Harbinger, Masland
Fabrics: Knoll

Ceilings: Armstrong
General Contractors: Turner Construction Company
Lighting Consultants: Jerry Kugler Associates

Vanderbilt University, Sarratt Student Center
Design Firm: Bruner/Cott
Carpets & Flooring: Lees
Fabrics: Architex
Lighting: Elliptipar, Lightolier, Lithonia
Ceilings: Armstrong
Wallcoverings and Paint: Porter Paints
Window Treatments: Levolor
General Contractors: DF Chase Construction
Lighting Consultants: LAM Lighting Consultants

West Virginia University, Life Sciences Building
Design Firm: Payette
Furniture: Haworth, Knoll
Carpets & Flooring: Armstrong, Bolyu, Karastan
Fabrics: Knoll, Maharam
Ceilings: Armstrong
Wallcoverings and Paint: Quron
General Contractors: Dick Corporation
Lighting Consultants: BR+A Consulting Engineers

NeoCon® SHOWS

North America's **largest** collection of expositions and conferences for interior design and facilities management ...

NeoCon® Shows

NeoCon®
World's Trade
Fair

IIDEX®/NeoCon®
Canada

NeoCon® East

NeoCon® Xpress

TECHNOLOGY • WORKPLACE • HEALTHCARE • RETAIL • HOSPITALITY • RESIDENTIAL • FLOORCOVERING • LIGHTING • ARCHITECTURAL PRODUCTS • WORKPLACE • SUSTAINABLE DESIGN

SUSTAINABLE DESIGN • WORKPLACE • ARCHITECTURAL PRODUCTS • LIGHTING • FLOORCOVERING • RESIDENTIAL • HOSPITALITY • RETAIL • HEALTHCARE • WORKPLACE • TECHNOLOGY

IIDEX®/NeoCon® Canada
September 28-29, 2006
The National Trade Centre
Toronto, Ont.

NeoCon® East
October 11-12, 2006
Baltimore Convention Center
Baltimore, Md.

NeoCon® World's Trade Fair
June 11-13, 2007
The Merchandise Mart • Chicago, Ill.

NeoCon® Xpress
September 2007
Los Angeles, Calif.

photography by | audia • john dean • felderman keatinge & associates • steve reisch

www.merchandisemart.com 800.677.6278

Index by Project